JESUS
is the
G.O.A.T.

JESUS
is the
G.O.A.T.

Life lessons from the Greatest of All Time

DR. JAMES BLEWETT

Printed in the United States of America
ISBN 978-1-958434-13-0 (sc)
ISBN 978-1-958434-14-7 (e)

Library of Congress Control Number: 2022909513

2022.05.27

MainSpring Books
5901 W. Century Blvd
Suite 750
Los Angeles, CA, US, 90045

www.mainspringbooks.com

TABLE OF CONTENTS

Introduction vii

Chapter 1   Jesus is the greatest example of all time 1

Chapter 2   Jesus is the greatest teacher of all time. 15

Chapter 3   Jesus is the greatest story teller of all time. 31

Chapter 4   Jesus is the greatest hope of all time 50

Chapter 5   Jesus is the greatest Savior of all time 65

Chapter 6   Now What? 87

Endnotes 91

INTRODUCTION

"We cannot too often or too plainly tell the seeking soul that his only hope for salvation lies in the Lord Jesus Christ. It lies in Him completely, only, and alone. To save both from the guilt and the power of sin, Jesus is sufficient. His name is called Jesus, because He shall save His people from their sin."

– Charles Spurgeon[1]

As young kid growing up in Florida in the 90s I was a huge basketball fan. I could play basketball all day, and then I would talk about basketball when I wasn't playing, and finally I would watch basketball at night. With the very basic cable package we got WGN, as did all of my friends. This means I got a front row seat to the most amazing, talented, and decorated basketball player of all time: His Airness, Michael Jordan.

Not everybody understands what G.O.A.T. means, to me you look no further than number 23 if you want to know what it looks like to be the Greatest Of All Time. I had a parent call me once time because her daughter called her a goat and she was too embarrassed to ask her what it meant, but wanted to make sure she shouldn't be offended. I assured her, that her teenage daughter just paid her the highest compliment that a teenager can give, not by calling her a goat, but by calling her G.O.A.T.

I spent many nights watching Michael Jordan play when I was little and I just remember saying "Wow" over and over again. I understand that even though Jordan was definitely the G.O.A.T. of my generation that maybe Lebron or Kobe or Steph would be considered the G.O.A.T. of another.

Before my time, some would argue Kareem Abdul Jabar or Oscar Robertson to be the G.O.A.T. for them.

In football we have discussions about whether Joe Montana or Tom Brady or someone else is the G.O.A.T. The golf experts have been trying to decide for a lot of years whether or not Tiger Woods or Jack Nicklaus is the G.O.A.T. These debates have been had at sports bars and company break rooms for a very long time and will probably continue on forever.

But even though we may disagree on who the G.O.A.T. is from generation to generation when it comes to sports, one truth remains, Jesus is the G.O.A.T. for all time and for all generations. Jesus is the most influential person in the history of the world.

I want to propose to you in this book that Jesus is the greatest of all time and there will never be a time where He is not the greatest. In Luke 9:43 "And they were all amazed at the greatness of God."

The thing about Michael Jordan is that no one will ever convince me that anyone is any greater than him because I have a personal connection to his career. I watched every game of his 72-10 record setting season with my grandmother in her living room. It was our bonding time, it was our special thing that we had.

On March 24, 1996 the Chicago Bulls lost for only the eighth time that year. That morning I attended First Baptist Church of Tampa for the first time and on Tuesday of that week, I got a visit from the youth pastor of the church and I accepted Jesus into my heart. It was on that night that I realized that while Michael Jordan was fun to watch, he could not save me from my sins.

I decided from that point on that I would talk about Jesus with the same enthusiasm that I would talk about Air Jordan. Nobody can ever convince me that Jesus is not the greatest of all time because He has changed my life. My goal is that by the end of this book you will see the exact same thing and He will change your life too.

We will look at Jesus as the greatest example of all time, the greatest teacher of all time, the greatest storyteller of all time, the greatest hope of all time, and the greatest Savior of all time. In other words, He is the Greatest of All Time. Jesus is the G.O.A.T.

CHAPTER ONE

Jesus is the greatest example of all time.

"Interest in Jesus Himself is of preeminent importance. The mystery of His Person, the graciousness of His teaching, the beauty of His character, the wonder of His deeds, all these are of such value that it is impossible to attend to them too closely, or to write too much concerning them."

–Morgan, G. Campbell

When Michael Jordan played basketball everyone wanted to emulate him. When Tiger Woods was at the top of his golf game, everyone wanted to hit a driver like he did. It is natural to be like the greatest. With Jesus it is no different, our goal should not be "I wanna be like Mike" it should be "I wanna be like Jesus."

The ironic thing about athletes and other famous people is that people want to be like them and yet those very people would advise against it. Even though Jordan had an ad campaign that said "I wanna be like Mike", he would still say that he was not to be anybody's role model. You could try to be like M.J. on the basketball court and wear the clothes that he wants you to wear, but would very much prefer it if you didn't follow his *example*.

This is where we leave the discussion of idolizing a sports star and move it to emulating a Savior. Jesus wants us to follow His example, He wants us to model our lives after Him, He wants us to surrender His leading. In fact, Paul sums up the entire Christian life so well when He says in 1 Corinthians to " Follow my example, as I follow the example of Christ."

Therefore, if we are to follow the example of Christ, we must understand the mindset of Christ. Jesus differs greatly from most of the celebrities we adore because He clothes Himself in humility. And the fact we follow a humble leader means that we need to have a humble mindset.

Phil. 2:5-8 "5 Have this attitude in yourselves which was also in Christ Jesus, 6 who, although He existed in the form of God, did not regard equality with God a thing to be grasped, 7 but emptied Himself, taking the form of a bond-servant, and being made in the likeness of men. 8 Being found in appearance as a man, He humbled Himself by becoming obedient to the point of death, even death on a cross."

It is this mindset of humility that we will be looking at as we establish the fact that Jesus is the greatest example of all time . . . but . . . before we get too serious, let's have a little fun. You see, I should start out by discussing the discipline it took for Him to be who He was. Or I should start with the difficulties He had to endure. Maybe even the dedication He had to have. But, that's not a fun way to start a book.

The best way to start this book of is with a PARTY! Let's look at Jesus the Dinner Guest. In John chapter 2 we find the first recorded miracle of Jesus, and it happened at a party - a wedding to be exact. Let that sink in for a minute. It's okay to have a little fun as a follower of Jesus, after all, He is setting the example.

Christians often are accused of being people who don't like to have fun. A lot of times we have earned this moniker. I've often been amazed at how crazy and ridiculous grown men get at a college football game and how those same people will stare me down in church for clapping too loud after a baptism. God does not hate fun and He does not want us to hate it either. Some of the most fun that you can have is when you are together in a social setting with people you love.

John records 7 signs (7 total miracles Jesus performed) in his book and this is the very first one, and it happens to be at a wedding. The very last one happens at a funeral. The very first one is mostly kept private. The very last one is a public spectacle. The very first one begins His ministry. The very last one all but ends it.

When we look at the story of John 2 at the wedding at Cana, the first thing that always sticks out to me is that someone was smart enough to invite Jesus to the party. Jesus accepted the invitation, although, He just recruited some of His disciples so He rolled up in that party with a "plus 7", no wonder they ran out of wine.

My wife and I got married on a tight budget. We both had full-time jobs and then we worked a ton of side jobs to save up money for our wedding. We cleaned carpets on the weekends, babysat at night, and even joined a catering crew a couple times for a few extra dollars.

Heather found an inexpensive, but beautiful, wedding dress. We got married in our beautiful church in downtown Tampa, but since we are Southern Baptist there was no dancing allowed at the reception. (Remember that Christians don't like to have fun thing.) So we did what most Southern Baptist couples do, we had the ceremony at the church and we drove somewhere else for the reception.

The funny thing is that our reception was actually a whole lot more like a church potluck than a wedding reception. We had all sorts of food in a buffet line, and most of it was brought by people we knew. We could only afford to rent the clubhouse we were at for two hours, so after our traditional first dance, and after we cut the cake, and after Uncle Leroy got his second helping of Aunt Betty's lasagna, we had to kick people out. We couldn't afford to pay the penalty for going over.

So when Jesus walks in with seven unexpected guests, I can totally understand why this would be a problem. If seven extra people came to my wedding there would not have been enough of cousin Gretta's deviled eggs left for everyone. This is the problem that this wedding feast was running into with wine.

As a result of this problem, we see an interesting interaction between Jesus and His mom. His mom wants Him to turn the water into wine, and you can almost read the tone into this story that she asked in the same way she asked Him to clean His room. So Jesus did what His mom asked. He turned the water into wine and only the disciples that were with Him, His mom and some servants knew what happened.

The wine was then presented to the Master of the Feast. (When I visualize this story I picture that the Master of the Feast as Martin Short in Father of the Bride.) So the guy with the coolest job title in the whole Bible drinks the wine and declares it better than the wine before it. Which just shows us that Jesus is here to provide fullness in our lives and that fullness is better than anything else out there.

Have you ever wondered why this is the first miracle performed by Jesus? It has a lot to do with the jars. John 2:6 says, "Now there were six stone waterpots set there for the Jewish custom of purification, containing twenty or thirty gallons each." Jesus used the pots from the ceremonial cleaning to signify that they would no longer be used for cleansing because He is about to usher in a brand new age. The Old Covenant is about to go away and He is about to bring something completely new.

The Jewish ceremonial cleansing was to externally cleanse the Jewish people to make them pure before God. Jesus was about to bring about change, where He was going to cleanse people from within and it would last for all time. The Jewish people were God's chosen people and were at that point married to God. But soon, Jesus would die for us all and all that accept Him as their Savior will become the bride of Christ. This is why the wedding scene is so significant.

Moses was someone who personified the Old Covenant. When Moses performed his first miracle, he turned water into blood which represented judgment. When Jesus performed His first miracle He turned water into wine which represented joy. Jesus set the example right off the bat that we are to be people of fullness and joy.

So when people think of Christians as people who only judge, they are inaccurate. Jesus demonstrates to us through this miracle that the Christian life is not about judgement but about joy. How about that for an example to follow?

We can see Jesus as a **dinner guest** and that was certainly a good way to start out, but now we must move on to Jesus' **discipline.** I think back to some of these athletes that I've mentioned already. I think back to Michael Jordan winning 6 NBA championships. I think back to Tiger Woods winning 15 Major tournament's. I, of course, also think to Tom Brady and his 6 Super Bowl trophies (and counting.) I think these guys have been invited to a lot of parties to celebrate their success, but they would tell you that it is the preparation that leads to the party.

The heart of a champion is that even when the season is over, you are still training. It is the weights lifted over the Summer, the thousand free throws a day, and the countless hours spent on the driving range that leads a champion to have success. In other words, it takes discipline. This is another area where Jesus has set the greatest example of all time.

Jesus did three things that stood out as a means of preparation for his Earthly ministry. He spent time in solitude, worship, and prayer. As our example these are things that we must make disciplines in our own lives.

There are many instances in the Bible wherein Jesus gets up and leaves everyone to be alone. If we are truly to be like Christ then this practice is one that we should not overlook.

All four gospels give an example of Jesus being in solitude
Matthew 14:13 is one time.

> *13 Now when Jesus heard about John, He withdrew from there in a boat to a secluded place by Himself; and when the people heard of this, they followed Him on foot from the cities.*[2]

Mark 1:35 is another example.

> *35 In the early morning, while it was still dark, Jesus got up, left the house, and went away to a secluded place, and was praying there.*

And in Luke 5:16

> *16 But Jesus Himself would often slip away to the wilderness and pray.*[3]

And John's gospel records it in John 6:15.

> *15 So Jesus, perceiving that they were intending to come and take Him by force to make Him king, withdrew again to the mountain by Himself alone.*[4]

I would imagine that being around all of the crowds that he was around and even spending so much time with his twelve disciples, that just having a time to be by himself was very important. But what were the other reasons He went to be by himself. I believe He had this practice to recharge spiritually and emotionally, to gain the right perspective, to learn to do spiritual battle, and to listen to God.

Jay Dennis says in his book <u>Jesus Habits</u>[5] that "The Jesus habit of seclusion is withdrawing, momentarily or for an extended period of time, from everyday noise and demands, to spend some time with God for the purpose of connecting with God and allowing your emotional and spiritual batteries to be recharged. This is time built into your daily schedule, no matter how busy and complicated that schedule might be."

Worship was also another habit that Jesus had in order to prepare Himself to be the greatest example of all time. Jesus worshipped God both privately and corporately. What a statement that is. Jesus, who is God, made it a habit and a part of his everyday life to worship God.

In Matthew 26 when Jesus was being confronted by his adversaries He said

> *55 At that time Jesus said to the crowds, "Have you come out with swords and clubs to arrest Me as you would against a robber? Every day I used to sit in the temple teaching and you did not seize Me."*[6]

Every day is a whole lot different than once a week or on Christmas and Easter, and Jesus made it very clear just how often He corporately worshipped. So GO TO CHURCH. But don't just go to church, go to church expectantly.

I've witnessed many times in my years as a Christian where the expectation of the participant has led to the desired outcome. Let me give you an example of what I mean. Suzy gets out of bed on a Sunday morning and is dreading going to church. Lucy gets out of bed eagerly anticipating going to church.

Suzy and Lucy sit together on the same pew, sing the same songs, hear the same sermon and eat at the same lunch table when it is all over. Suzy complains about how awful everything was and how terrible the sermon was. Lucy, on the other hand, was convinced that she had just been to one of the best worship services she had ever attended and she felt so much closer to God because of it. What is the difference? Expectations.

I've been a youth pastor for over 16 years and in my experience, this is the greatest benefit of Youth Camp. The youth gear themselves up all year that God is going to show up at Camp. Even though God shows up wherever two or more are gathered in His name, the students just notice Him more at Camp . . . because they are expecting to. Expectant worship is worshipping God and expecting for Him to speak to you, and He will.

Jesus also had a great passion about God's house. Of course the times when He turned over the table in the temple immediately comes to mind. But often overlooked is what His disciples were thinking during this time. It is recorded in John 2:17.

> *17 His disciples remembered that it was written, "ZEAL FOR YOUR HOUSE WILL CONSUME ME."[7]*

The disciples are remembering Psalm 69:9 during this time and Jesus' zeal for the house of God is extremely obvious. But the real interesting thing here is the connection to the wedding. If Jesus used the ceremonial cleansing pots to let us know that the old way is not going to work anymore, I would say that that is what He was doing in the temple as well.

In the book of John these two events happen right after each other; the miracle at the wedding, and the turning over of tables in the Temple. The wedding was Jesus setting the example that He is the new sacrifice, Him overturning the tables in the temple was Jesus setting the example that He is the new temple. He was letting them know (and us as well) that He was about to usher in the new covenant and He would be our temple. He would be the way that we gain approval with God.

So in order to follow his example we need to practice the disciplines He had. Jesus practiced seclusion, had consistent worship, and of course, had a very fervent prayer life.

A lot of people think that prayer is reserved for those times in life when things are falling apart. They are like, "Okay I am running late, I am going to be in trouble . . . God I really need you to bail me out on this one."

Prayer is not to be our insurance policy. Some people think that prayer is reserved for those times in your life, when you just can't handle things for yourself anymore. While God will occasionally answer those prayers, that is not the purpose of prayer.

In order to fully grasp the purpose and meaning of prayer as taught and emulated by Jesus we need to go back to the Old Testament and start with the priests. In the Old Testament the priests were holy people who performed a lot of holy duties. They were in charge of performing sacred duties in and around the tabernacle.

But then there was the high priest, and the first high priest was Aaron. And the high priest's job description involves being the only one who is able to go into the Holy of Holies, and he could only do it once a year or else he would DIE. The only time that he could enter the Holy of Holies was once a year on a day called the Day of Atonement.

But he couldn't just stroll on into the Holy of Holies like he was just walking into church, he had to prepare himself. This goes back to the water jars that we found at the wedding, a representation of the Old Covenant.

People still prayed in the Old Testament, but they weren't granted full access to God. They couldn't just talk to God anytime they wanted to; there were conditions that went along with it. The only ones who were granted access to God were the priests and in the Old Testament that would have been the Levites. And of course, the high priests had even more access.

Have you ever downloaded a "free" app for your phone only to find that it's not really free. You can get to the title screen and everything loads, but then you press a button to do something and it wants to charge you $1.99. The problem is that even though you have downloaded the app, you don't have complete access. That is the way prayer was in the Old Testament.

So let's fast forward to the New Testament. Jesus hit the scene and hit it hard. He kept on teaching things that people didn't understand, but ultimately the plan was beautiful. He was to be the offering. He was going to be OUR HIGH PRIEST and enter the only place more holy than the Holy of Holies. He was to enter Heaven, the very presence of God, and He was to make a sacrifice, but this time not with bulls or goats, this time the sacrifice was a human one. He sacrificed himself as the perfect sacrifice, and the eternal sacrifice. And when Jesus breathed His last breath, the book of Mark says that the curtain to the temple that surrounded the Holy of Holies was torn from top to bottom, and that curtain was the one that separated God from the rest of us.

So what does that mean for us? That means that now we have full access to God. This is how Jesus described it in John 16:22-24.

> 22 *"Therefore you too have grief now; but I will see you again, and your heart will rejoice, and no one will take your joy away from you. 23 "In that day you will not question Me about anything. Truly, truly, I say to you, if you ask the Father for anything in My name, He will give it to you. 24 "Until now you have asked for nothing in My name; ask and you will receive, so that your joy may be made full.*[8]

When my son Ethan was almost four, he started going through a stage where he thought there were monsters in his room. Sometimes he would wake up in the middle of the night and come into my room and I would hold him and soothe him. I would then go check for the monsters under his bed, usually I wouldn't find any. I would then tuck him back into bed and send him back to sleep. But I would still tell him that he could come into my room and wake me any time he wanted to if he was still scared.

I have an intern that works with me whose name is also James. James graduated from college and has a very bright future as a Pastor and I value my relationship with James. We are definitely brothers in Christ.

BUT . . . If James ever came to my house in the middle of the night and came into my room where I was sleeping and asked me to comfort him because he was scared . . . I would call the cops. I would yell at him to get out of my room and get out of my house and I would certainly not be too thrilled with him when he got to work the next day.

What is the difference between the two? One has full access to me and one only has partial access to me. Because Ethan is my son he has full access to me at any time and any place . . . James does not.

And the amazing thing is that we have that kind of access to God; any time, any place. Make sure you take advantage of that. Jesus gave us permission. He said, "Look, I am your high priest, so just mention my name and you can get in." That is why we always say at the end of our prayers, in Jesus' name, because we have been given that access.

I think knowing this, we should understand a lot more clearly the importance of prayer. Think about it, in the Old Testament you had to be cleansed and sacrifice animals and spin around three times in a circle, solve a Sudoku puzzle, say your alphabet backwards and then one person can go in once a year to have full access to God, and if they didn't follow that to the T then they would DIE.

So this paints a picture to lead to this point, if Jesus (the one who made every day prayer possible) prays how much more should we. And in preparation for every part of His ministry Jesus prayed.

One of the most poignant times was when Jesus was in the garden and He was praying. He prayed this, "If at all possible let this cup pass from me, but not my will but your will be done." This is the paradox of Jesus praying: Jesus, as God in human form, was praying to God the Father to ask that if it's possible that the cup would pass from Him, but if not, let it be done.

This is a beautiful prayer and one that can personally revolutionize our prayer lives. A lot of times our prayer life just consists of reading off a list, or you will get the ole' "God you know the prayer requests . . . so answer them please." How much more powerful would our prayer lives be if knowing that we are a priest of God with all authority in Heaven and Earth given to you from the high priest himself? If you would pray, "God please heal my cousin who is in the hospital right now and struggling. But God if not please help me understand why. And his family too." That will revolutionize your prayer life.

And that is the example Jesus gave when He prayed. But the question is still a little bit perplexing as to why Jesus prayed. Philip Yancey put it best in his book called Prayer, Does it Make a Difference?[9] When he said:

"Jesus seemed fully at ease with the Father and at unease with the world. For Him, prayer provided a refreshing reminder of cosmic reality, the 'view from above' so often obscured on planet Earth. Sometimes Jesus reminisced about that hidden realm: praying at supper the night of his arrest he recalled 'the glory I had with you before the world began.' Occasionally he felt such frustration with conditions on earth that He would let loose with a sigh: 'O unbelieving generation . . . how long shall I put up with you?' Jesus came from a place where God's command met no opposition; he knew exactly what He was asking when He instructed us to pray: 'your will be done on earth as it is in Heaven."

Therefore, if we are going to follow the greatest example of all time, we should accept the invitation to be a **dinner guest,** we should emulate His **disciplines**, which were that Jesus definitely utilized prayer as an asset as well as solitude and worship. However, we must also follow His example through **difficulties.**

When you think of the life of a pro athlete, you know that there are a lot of difficulties that come along with being one. There are some things that we know about as the general public and some things that we will never know about.

I think back to the 1997-98 season of the Chicago Bulls. Michael Jordan and his teammates were trying to win the organization's sixth championship. Scottie Pippen got hurt early on and the Bulls had to figure out how to perform well without him. Phil Jackson was coaching for his last season and there was complications with being a lame duck coach. And everywhere Jordan went, and every city that he travelled to, he was asked the same question, "Are you coming back next year?"

So while difficulties might include injuries and accusations and internal drama, there are also other things that are classified as difficulties. In the Christian life, we summarize these difficulties as temptations and trials. One of the other reasons we can follow Jesus' example is because He was able to show people that temptations and trials can be overcome. He shows us what it is like to grow through our **difficulties.** The first way that He showed this to us was through the temptation. This is when Jesus' earthly ministry actually began.

Some believe Jesus' earthly ministry began when Jesus turned water into wine at the request of His mother for His first miracle. Some believe that Jesus' ministry began when He was baptized by John the Baptist. R.C. Sproul is one of those people.

When Jesus entered the Jordan River to be baptized by John, this event marked the beginning of Jesus' earthly ministry. Here He not only identified Himself with the sin of His people, He was also anointed by the Holy Spirit for ministry. In a sense this was Jesus' ordination. Here He began His vocation as the Christ."[10] However, it can also be argued that Jesus' ministry began after all of these events, because Jesus still needed to receive power.

One could actually make a logical case that His ministry actually didn't begin until after the temptation of Christ by Satan. This is when Scripture indicates that Jesus received His power. This coincides with what is written later on in the New Testament in the book of James.

James 1:2-4 says *"Consider it all joy, my brethren, when you encounter various trials, knowing that the testing of your faith produces endurance. And let endurance have its perfect result, so that you may be perfect and complete, lacking in nothing."*[11]

I don't particularly like this verse. I would like it much better if it read: Consider it all joy, my brethren, when you encounter various buffets, knowing that the eating of your prime rib covered in mac and cheese next to a mountain of mashed potatoes produces endurance. Unfortunately, it does not say that though. We WILL go through various trials and it is through these trials that we can follow Jesus' example.

After Jesus' baptism in the Jordan River the Bible describes it this way in Luke 4:1: *"Jesus, full of the Holy Spirit, returned from the Jordan and was led around by the Spirit in the wilderness"*[12]

So now Jesus is "full" of the Holy Spirit. The Greek word is "pleres" [Strong's 4134][13] and it means complete. And the very next thing that happens after the baptism of Jesus was the temptation of Jesus and Luke 4:1 very clearly states that it is actually the Spirit that "led" Him there. The Greek word for led is the word "ago" [Strong's 71][14] and it is a physical leading of someone. It is actually the same word used in Matthew 27:31 during the crucifixion of Jesus. *"After they had mocked Him, they took the scarlet robe off Him and put His own garments back on Him, and led Him away to crucify Him."*[15]

The Spirit is leading Jesus into the temptation. Jesus overcomes everything that was thrown at Him. Satan tempts Him three times and all three times Jesus uses the book of Deuteronomy to combat the temptation of Satan and then Jesus is on the other side of the temptation and this is how it is described in Luke 4:14. *"And Jesus returned to Galilee in the power of the Spirit, and news about Him spread through all the surrounding district. And He began teaching in their synagogues and was praised by all."*[16]

He returns in the POWER of the Spirit. The word power here is the Greek word "dunamos"[17] and it is where the modern term dynamite comes from. So Jesus goes from being "full" of the Spirit, to being "led" by the Spirit, to being in the "power" of the Spirit, and as soon as He goes through this progression the Bible immediately says that "He began teaching in the synagogues"[18]

What we find then through this example is that if we truly want to walk in the power of the Holy Spirit, we are going to have to encounter difficulties. Difficulties are what God uses to refine us, because in these moments we have to rely on Him.

The last thing we must look at if we are going to follow the greatest example of all time is His **dedication.** Each year as Tiger Woods would go out to the golf course, he would think about being the best. That is what he wanted, to be the best golfer in the whole world. He was dedicated to this goal.

The dedication of Jesus is found in the way He interacts with people. Jesus was dedicated to the goal of showing us that we are to love one another. The interaction that I would like to begin with is His interaction with Zacchaeus. The story of Zacchaeus found in Luke 19. [19]

This particular story is part of what is called Jesus' travelling narrative. This is a collection of things Jesus did as He was going from place to place. In other words, no matter how busy things got or how impatient Peter became, Jesus would stop and do ministry and thereby teach us through example the way we are to traverse our overly busy lives.

In the midst of one of His travels, Jesus stops to notice a man that the Bible describes as having a lot of money, having a job that would make no one like him, and that he was short. It also said that this man climbed a tree to see Jesus, and this was a very inappropriate thing to do during this day and age. And yet this is exactly what this man did, and Jesus responded by looking at him.

It is at this point that if you went to church as a child you start singing the "Zacchaeus was a wee little man" song in your head. And when you get to the part that says, "Zacchaeus, you come down!" I assume you use the hand motion that goes with the song and you wag your finger at this imaginary midget on a branch. But I think this is a dangerous thing to teach children and a dangerous way to view Jesus.

I don't believe Jesus wagged His finger at all, I believe Jesus looked at Zacchaeus with love and compassion, and if any hand motions should be used it would be arms spread wide open ready to embrace His new vertically challenged friend as He got down from that tree. And this very act changed the life of Zacccchaeus and a lot of people around him because Jesus was willing to look at him.

Matthew Henry says of Zaccheaus that "His name bespeaks him a Jew. Zaccai was a common name among the Jews; they had a famous rabbi, much about this time, of that name."[20] He also says this about his financial situation, "The inferior publicans were commonly men of broken fortunes, and low in the world; but he was chief of the publicans had raised a good estate. Christ had lately shown how hard it is for rich people to enter into the kingdom of God yet presently produces an instance of one rich man that had been lost, and was found, and that not as the prodigal by being reduced to want."[21]

I think the most important thing in this story is that when Jesus called Zaccheus down from the tree, He called him by name. He didn't call him sinner, or tax collector, or short guy . . . He called him by His actual name. Jesus is calling your name too.

If you are reading this book right now it might be because you desperately want to see Jesus. Right now, Jesus is calling you by your name . . . and He loves you. You. Just as you are.

Now our job is to follow the example of Jesus and become dedicated to seeing other people, even ones that seem "unloveable" and show them the love that Jesus shows you.

Jesus taught us how we are to interact with people, no matter what they have done; with love, respect, and compassion. We will see in the next chapter that He teaches us so much more than just that.

CHAPTER TWO

Jesus is the greatest teacher of all time.

"People often ask when the next step in evolution—the step to something beyond man—will happen. But in the Christian view, it has happened already. In Christ a new kind of man appeared: and the new kind of life which began in Him is to be put into us."

– *C.S. Lewis*[22]

D o you remember your favorite teacher from school? Some of us have some real fond memories of a few of our teachers, and some not-so-good memories of some others.

I can remember when I was in High School that we gave our Spanish teacher a real hard time. She didn't speak much English, so we could rally the troops behind her back without her knowing. There was one time when she stepped out of the room and everyone turned their desks around while she was gone. There was also the time that, in unison, the class stood up to give the Pledge of Allegiance while she was in the middle of teaching the proper use for the word "usted". How did she respond? She faced the flag with her hand over her heart, of course.

My wife is a phenomenal teacher. I've had the privilege of being a Pastor where she was teaching at the Christian school for years. I can remember one time in particular that I walked into her classroom unannounced, only to see her rapping the alphabet to her Kindergarten students. She was better than Kanye.

So whether you have had real good teachers in your life, or some that have been not so "bueno", we all can understand the importance of a good teacher. I can argue, pretty convincingly, that when it comes to being a teacher that Jesus is the greatest teacher of all time. The thing about His teachings though, is that they didn't take place in a classroom. Jesus taught to the **masses**, to the **marginalized**, through **miracles**, and even while He was in **misery**.

So let's start with the masses. Jesus' most popular teaching time was when He delivered the Sermon on the Mount. The sermon on the mount was delivered early on in the ministry of Jesus and the main point of the sermon was to give hope to the hopeless. This may be why St. Augustine said "anyone who piously and earnestly ponders the Sermon on the Mount — as we read in the Gospel according to Mathew — I believe he will find therein . . . the perfect standard of the Christian Life."[23]

In regards to the sermon on the mount, Charles M. Crowe says, ". . . Jesus does not set up some detailed doctrine for human thinking nor a definite plan for conduct. He seeks to impart a divine, human quality of life that is different from the earthy ordinary. The Sermon is a message designed to make life winsome, brave, free, and full."[24] In other words, it is designed to bring hope to the hopeless.

The main point of this sermon is found in Matthew 5:17:[25] *"Do not think that I came to abolish the Law or the Prophets; I did not come to abolish but to fulfill."* No one really knows how much the audience actually understood about this concept, however in hindsight it is apparent that Jesus was bringing hope to the hopeless through this statement.

John Calvin was referring to this verse when he said: "Christ, therefore, now declares, that his doctrine is so far from being at variance with the law, that it agrees perfectly with the law and the prophets, and not only so, but brings the complete fulfillment of them."[26] This goes to show that when Moses first came to bring the law and when Elijah prophesied to his people, that one day Jesus was to come to fulfill and complete all of the things that, through God, they had begun.

Jesus, through the Sermon on the Mount, was establishing a foundation for the people to let them know that as hard as they try they will never be perfect, and thus they are a people in desperate need of a Savior. Jesus came to be that Savior.

So Jesus starts out this sermon by giving the Beatitudes found in Matthew 5:3-10[27]

> *"Blessed are the poor in spirit, for theirs is the kingdom of heaven. 4 "Blessed are those who mourn, for they shall be comforted. 5 "Blessed are the gentle, for they shall inherit the earth. 6 "Blessed are those who hunger and thirst for righteousness, for they shall be satisfied. 7 "Blessed are the merciful, for they shall receive mercy. 8 "Blessed are the pure in heart, for they shall see God. 9 "Blessed are the peacemakers, for they shall be called sons of God. 10 "Blessed are those who have been persecuted for the sake of righteousness, for theirs is the kingdom of heaven.*

According to James Forest in <u>The Ladder of Beatitude</u>[28] "The term beatitude comes from the Latin adjective beātitūdō which means "happy", "fortunate", or "blissful". In the Vulgate (Latin), the book of Matthew titles this section Beatitudines, and "Beatitudes" was anglicized from that term."

Jesus was always doing things differently than everyone expected Him to. Jesus was always teaching on things like loving your enemies and praying for those who persecute you, and this was different than anything anybody had ever heard. So when Jesus spoke everyone wanted to listen and the beatitudes were how he started out this sermon.

Therefore when Jesus says "Blessed are the poor in spirit, because the kingdom of Heaven is theirs." It is so hard to understand. Because those that are poor in spirit certainly don't feel very blessed. And one of the most confounding of the Beatitudes is found in Matthew 5:4[29] and it says "Blessed are those who mourn, because they will be comforted."

The definition of mourn is to feel sadness.[30] The actual Greek word for this in the Bible is pentheo[31]. Paul understood this Beatitude well when he wrote in 2 Corinthians 1:3-7[32]:

"Praise be to the God and Father of our Lord Jesus Christ, the Father of compassion and the God of all comfort, who comforts us in all our troubles, so that we can comfort those in any trouble with the comfort we ourselves have received from God. For just as the sufferings of Christ flow over into our lives, so also through Christ our comfort overflows. If we are distressed, it is for your comfort and salvation; if we are comforted, it is for your comfort, which produces in you patient endurance of the same sufferings we suffer. And our hope for you is firm, because we know that just as you share in our sufferings, so also you share in our comfort."

These verses say that God is the God of all Comfort. During the troubles of His people, he comforts them. These verses go on and on about how to be comforted. Notice these verses don't say that God will make our circumstances different, but he will comfort us through them. This is one of the ways that Jesus' teachings is bringing hope to the hopeless.

When the Bible mentions this idea of comfort, I always seem to think of Charles Schultz and the old Peanuts gang. In the Peanuts gang was a boy named Linus, and Linus is infamously known for one thing: his blanket. Linus always traveled around with his blanket. Always.

I believe the reason Linus always had his blanket was because he needed the security, he needed the comfort. Whenever anything went wrong for Linus he had to hold onto his blanket even more, he held it close and he held onto it real tight. Linus could never get through tough situations unless he had his blanket with him.

The message that I believe Jesus is teaching through what I believe is the most difficult beatitude to grasp is: just like Linus needed his security blanket to get through tough times, so we should cling to God. We need to keep Him close and hold him really close, because God is the God of all comfort.

This is why the great theologian Jonathan Edwards said, "when it is thus with Christians, their trouble is commonly greatly increased a little before the renewal of hope and comfort. When sin prevails, as has been said, in the hearts of Christians, they are not wont to be easy and quiet like secure sinners."[33] This comfort that Jesus speaks about in the Beatitudes goes right along with the hope that he brings to the hopeless.

Jesus said a lot of seemingly backwards things when He gave the sermon on the mount. Jesus also said some things that were more metaphorical in nature. Jesus told the audience that they are the light of the world and the salt of the Earth.

The light of the world one can be interpreted by noticing the difference between light and darkness. Darkness is evil and light is good. It only takes a little bit of light to drown out the darkness but a whole lot of light completely kills the darkness. This would have been something that equated to people of that day, and hearing this great teacher tell them that they could drown out darkness would have filled them with hope.

Nowadays, I think we can relate to this concept by talking about our cell phone light. If you are ever the last person to go to bed, you always have to perform the perfect ballet in order to turn all the lights off in the right order so you don't trip over anything on the way to your bed. If you are smart, you keep that cell phone close by, because even when the house is pitch black, if you turn on that cell phone light it can prevent you from bumping your big toe on that ottoman . . . again.

The world is very dark place. There are a lot of things for us to stumble on. But it just takes the smallest of lights to cancel out the darkness to help us find our way.

As far as the salt reference goes, to me it reminds me of french fries and high cholesterol, for people of that day it was used to preserve food. It was a hot commodity, because there was no refrigeration and salt was the only way they could eat something for more than one day and remain healthy doing so. So basically being the salt of the earth equates to a life-saving quality.

However, Stuart Briscoe in The Preacher's Commentary[34] had a more elaborate explanation for what Jesus meant when He called us the salt of the Earth.

> *"'You are the salt of the Earth' suggests at least three things: purity, preservation, and flavor. Salt in the Roman world symbolized purity—no doubt from the process of using sea water and the sun to acquire the salt. Roman soldiers were often paid in salt, the basis for the word "salary." Jesus' use of*

the symbol of salt to describe the disciple emphasizes the call and influence of purity the Christian brings to society. But salt was also a preservative in a day without refrigeration. This meaning is expressed in Jesus' warning about salt that has lost its savor (Luke 14:34–35). Meat spoiled unless it was salted. Similarly, the kingdom member is a preserving element in society. Salt loses itself in service to the object that is being salted or preserved, which is the third aspect of the meaning of this symbol—flavor. When salt is applied to food properly, it is not so that one can taste the salt, but so that the food itself tastes more authentically as it should. As salt makes the food more "foodier," the disciple as the salt of the earth makes the earth more authentically as it should be. Our role in society is not to be over against it so much as it is to enrich or purify the social order, making it more truly a realm of blessing for humanity. Such enriching persons are the salt of the earth."

Jesus then said a transitional phrase that had huge ramifications. He said that He came not to abolish the law but to keep it. He then proceeded to prove to the listeners that they were all people in desperate need of a Savior and He did this by showing them just how imperfect they really are.

Jesus went through the last five commandments of the Ten Commandments and upped the ante on all of them. He said that if you have anger in your heart, it is the same as murder. He said if you have ever looked lustfully at someone you have committed adultery. Thomas Aquinas noted, "not every society, much less every man, discovers the entire natural law, so God has revealed it in the Commandments so that it could be known with certainty by all men, of every society, and every age."[35]

Karl Barth says about this section of Scripture, "If the Ten Commandments state where [humanity] may and should stand before and with God, the Sermon on the Mount declares that [it] really has been placed there by God's own deed. If the Ten Commandments are a preface, the Sermon on the Mount is in a sense a postscript. The only question now is whether the church will live or not live in the fullness of life already granted to it."[36]

Jesus gave a lot of practical advice during this sermon as well. He gave advice on giving, fasting, prayer, money, anxiety, judging and many other things that we still use for the basis of our lives today. And then Jesus ends the greatest sermon ever with some of the most profound words ever uttered. The ending is found in Matthew 7:13-27[37]:

> *13 "Enter through the narrow gate; for the gate is wide and the way is broad that leads to destruction, and there are many who enter through it. 14 "For the gate is small and the way is narrow that leads to life, and there are few who find it.*

This is the point where Jesus offers to them the way of salvation. He says that wide is the gate that leads to destruction but narrow is the gate that leads to life. Jesus also says that the way lies were administered was through false prophets which Jesus warns against immediately following this statement as well as the initiator of all of this, Satan, who is the father of all lies.

John MacArthur refers to the statement of Jesus declaring there to be a wide and a narrow way by saying, "That is a provocative statement by our Lord. That is really the point to which He has been driving in all of the first part of this great, masterful sermon. He brings the whole thing to the climax of a decision, a choice. Two gates which bring the individual to two roads which lead to two destinations which are populated by two different crowds. The Lord then focuses on the inevitable decision that has to be made regarding that which He has been saying."[38]

Jesus then goes on to say that if you are truly saved then you will have fruit in your life. In other words there will be evidence of your salvation. But there are also going to be a lot of people who believe they are saved, but when they get to Heaven they will hear, "Depart from me, for I never knew you." And what a very sad thing that would be.

Jesus ends this sermon with a parable about building your house on the correct foundation. Because if you build your house on the wrong foundation it will fall to the ground when things get tough.

Albert Barnes in his commentary on the verse believed that Jesus use the metaphor of the foundation because it would have been very relatable to the people of that day. "Palestine was to a considerable extent a land of hills and mountains. Like other countries of that description, it was subject to sudden and violent rains. The Jordan, the principal stream, was annually swollen to a great extent, and became rapid and furious in its course. The streams which ran among the hills, whose channels might have been dry during some months of the year, became suddenly swollen with the rain, and would pour down impetuously into the plains below. Everything in the way of these torrents would be swept off. Even houses, erected within the reach of these sudden inundations, and especially if founded on sand or on any unsolid basis, would not stand before them."[39]

He believed that using this imagery was a great way of the master teacher getting His point across. He goes on to say "No comparison could, to a Jew, have been more striking."[40]

Verse 28 of this chapter reads,[41] "When Jesus had finished these words, the crowds were amazed at His teaching" The reason they were amazed is because through the whole sermon, as Jesus was laying the groundwork for the problem, the problem that existed within all of them, He also provided them a solution to the problem. The solution was the narrow gate of salvation through Christ alone, which filled them with hope they had never known before. In other words, He was proving to be the greatest teacher of all time.

So Jesus gave hope to this large crowd of people, but Jesus was also giving hope on a regular basis to people who were in need of a **miracle**. Jesus taught and modeled to love even those who are seemingly unlovely and Jesus modeled this for us in the way He interacted with other people. Jesus was willing to heal people, willing to touch people, and willing to look at people that society had all but written off, giving them hope that they had never received before.

An example of Jesus providing hope to someone in whom He healed is found in John 9:1-12.[42]

> *1 As He passed by, He saw a man blind from birth. 2 And His disciples asked Him, "Rabbi, who sinned, this man or his parents, that he would be born blind?" 3 Jesus answered, "It was neither that this man sinned, nor his parents; but it was so that the works of God might be displayed in him. 4 "We must work the works of Him who sent Me as long as it is day; night*

*is coming when no one can work. 5 "While I am in the world,
I am the Light of the world." 6 When He had said this, He
spat on the ground, and made clay of the spittle, and applied
the clay to his eyes, 7 and said to him, "Go, wash in the pool
of Siloam" (which is translated, Sent). So he went away and
washed, and came back seeing. 8 Therefore the neighbors, and
those who previously saw him as a beggar, were saying, "Is not
this the one who used to sit and beg?" 9 Others were saying,
"This is he," still others were saying, "No, but he is like him."
He kept saying, "I am the one." 10 So they were saying to him,
"How then were your eyes opened?" 11 He answered, "The
man who is called Jesus made clay, and anointed my eyes, and
said to me, 'Go to Siloam and wash '; so I went away and
washed, and I received sight." 12 They said to him, "Where is
He?" He said, "I do not know."*

First we notice that he was blind since birth. The Bible says that he was a man, which is to say that he was at least 30 years old. Then it says that he was a beggar. He couldn't work, so every day he'd find his way out into the street and beg for money or food. It also says that people looked down on him.

Charles Ellicott points out, about him being described as blind since birth, that "the fact was well known, and was probably publicly proclaimed by the man himself or his parents (John 9:20) as an aggravation of his misery, and as a plea for the alms of passers by. Of the six miracles connected with blindness which are recorded in the Gospels, this is the only case described as blindness from birth. In this lies its special characteristic, for "since the world began, was it not heard that any man opened the eyes of one that was born blind" (John 9:32)."[43]

In the blind man's society, he wasn't viewed with the same pity that would be granted to him now. He was the scum of the earth to those people. When you lose one of your senses, then the other senses are heightened. And the blind man wasn't deaf. He could hear the things that were being said about him. The criticism, the remarks, the jokes. He could hear the pace of the people's feet that were trying to avoid him. Every day, for 30 years he endured this.

To make matters worse, even the religious people in his day blamed him or his parents for his fate. You can see that even the disciples were thinking the same thing. They asked Jesus: "Who's to blame his parents or him?" If the disciples thought that, everyone else probably thought that too. Maybe even the blind man.

So where does this leave the blind man? The only hope that he might have had – God – was viewed as the person who was judging him for his sin. Later on in the story, his family is mentioned, but his family let him sit in the street and beg every day.

So here's the state of the blind man: He's been blind and begging for at least 30 years. Everyone despises him. He's ridiculed and insulted. Religious people give him no hope, because they blame him or his parents. God has judged him unmercifully by striking him with blindness, whether it was his fault or not, it would still seem cruel of God to do that to a human being.

For all these reasons, the blind man had every reason to believe that he would not be healed. Now enter Jesus into this whole situation. Jesus walks up close to where the Blind Man is, and spits on the ground.

The fact that Jesus spits on the ground in order to heal this man is very strange. There are two different times in which Jesus spit into the eyes of a blind man. This is the other one.

Mark 8:23-25[44]: "When they arrived at Bethsaida, they brought to him a blind man and begged him to touch him. He took the blind man by the hand and led him outside the village. Putting spittle on his eyes he laid his hands on him and asked, "Do you see anything?" Looking up he replied, "I see people looking like trees and walking." Then he laid hands on his eyes a second time and he saw clearly; his sight was restored and he could see everything distinctly.

Saliva was widely reported to have medicinal properties in the ancient world. For example, Celsus and Galen mention its healing properties and Pliny collected together many instances of its use in the treatment of boils, pains, sores, snake bites, epilepsy and eye disease. Plinio Prioreschi reports in A History of Medicine: Roman medicine, that the god told Vespasian to spit in the eyes of a blind man, who would thereby be cured.[45]

The people of that day knew that the saliva of a legitimate, first born heir would have healing properties against injury or disease. Having told the Pharisees that he was the legitimate son of God, all that remained was for him to demonstrate this by performing something that first-century Jews expected a legitimate, first born heir to do. Thus, maybe the spit is an affirmation that he is the only begotten son of God.

It also must be noted that the Augustine view on Jesus using spit might be a little different. "Augustine gives the mystical and allegorical explanation. He says that the spittle, which is saliva that descends from the head, signifies the Word of God, who proceeds from the Father, the head of all things: "I came forth from the mouth of the Most High" (Sir 24:3). Therefore, the Lord made clay from spittle and the earth when the Word was made flesh. He anointed the eyes of the blind man, that is, of the human race. And the eyes are the eyes of the heart, anointed by faith in the incarnation of Christ . . ." [46]

I think it is important to ask: How much spit? The dirt is very dry in the Middle East and the Bible describes the dirt as mud. Jesus was in the middle of a street, where it was more dry, and people and animals walking packed the earth down. Jesus was spitting a lot.

I don't think that even though Jesus was God that when He spit it was like a Super Soaker 6000. No, I think Jesus was spitting like crazy. I think it was a spectacle. I think people were stopping in their tracks and watching what Jesus was doing. I could just picture the disciples hiding behind a camel, or watching from a distance because they didn't want to look like idiots standing next to their teacher who was stirring up mud pies. Now this whole time, the blind man is sitting there listening. He could hear what was going on. He might have even been thinking, "What is this guy doing?!" Eventually, Jesus stopped and scooped up the saliva-soaked mud in his hands."

Now imagine the Blind Man: he knew exactly what was coming. He could hear the laughs of the people in the street, and some of the other people who were yelling "Gross!" I'm not sure how you say that in Arabic. And right there in that moment, the Blind Man had two choices: Obedience or Disobedience.

And I'm telling you he had every right in the world to say to Jesus: Listen, I have been blind and begged in this street for over 30 years. I have endured the criticism, ridicule, and hatred of the people who have stepped on and over me. Religious people have blamed me and my parents. For what? For some kind of sin? And my family they've abandoned me. They've left me to rot. God has shown nothing but cruelty to me. I don't want any part of this spectacle that you're trying to make of me, and I want no part of your God.

And to be honest with you, I wonder how many of us would have given that answer. Some of you may be thinking, oh I would have let Jesus put mud on me. How can we be sure? Have we spent 30 years of our lives like this guy did? Why would we have faith in something as bizarre as this, when in any one day, we don't even trust God enough to tell a friend about our relationship with God. How can we say that we would dare something so huge when we often don't believe the promises God has made and walk in faith to do the things that we know God has called us to do.

And it's an amazing thing when we apply our faith. You see, the blind man had no formal education, he had no religious training and yet people from all over were asking him to describe his views on this man named Jesus. And here was his answer; look I don't know about all of these things you are asking me about, here is what I do know, "I once was blind, but now I see." And that's how simple it is in your life, you don't have to have all the answers and you never will. All you have to tell people is that you once were blind but now you see.

So every day we're given two choices: we can walk in faith and watch God do the impossible and receive the prize or we can choose do just coast through life, and every time something seems a little risky or not 100% we can ease around it. We'll still be champions, but we will not have lived the Christian life of adventure that God had hoped for us. Jesus said, "I've come that you may have life and have it more abundantly." That life is all about living life on the edge. Seeing God show up when you're praying for someone for healing. Seeing God radically save and change one of your friend's lives when you dared to stare fear in the face and share your faith in Christ. That' the life that God has called us to. A life of adventure, a life of challenge, a life of fulfillment. And if your life is anything different than that, then you aren't experiencing the abundant life that Jesus wants for you.

Teaching to the masses and through miracles in the way Jesus did truly is amazing, but when it comes to Jesus being the G.O.A.T. as a teacher, nothing compares to the way that He was even teaching while He was in **misery**.

Jesus is betrayed, arrested, beaten, and forced to carry His cross to his ultimate Earthly demise. Even while hanging on that tree of torture Jesus managed to continue teaching. In fact, Jesus said seven things while He was hanging on the cross, which we know is the same number of days the world was created and it is commonly referred to as the number of completion.

The seven sayings form part of a Christian meditation that is often used during Lent, Holy Week and Good Friday. The traditional order of the sayings is Luke 23:34[47]: *Father, forgive them, for they do not know what they do.*

This saying is referred to as the word of forgiveness. It is amazing that even after all that Jesus has just been through; He is still teaching us to forgive. ". Jesus had proven his ability to forgive sins in his healing ministry (5:24). He had taught that forgiveness comes only to those who forgive others (6:37; 11:4) and that forgiveness has no limits (17:4). He had called for love of enemies (6:27-28). On the cross he practiced what he had taught. He watched those who mocked him, played games with him, scourged him, and crucified him. Then he asked the Father to forgive them[48]." How incredible.

He then interacts with the thieves on the cross, and tells one of them in Luke 23:43: *Truly, I say to you today, you will be with me in paradise.*[49]

This is known as the word of salvation and is a foundational statement for a lot of Christians. This is a statement that shows us that works cannot be a part of your salvation if a criminal is granted salvation with no good works to speak of under his belt. This is also a text read a lot at the bedsides of dying people to assure them that it is never too late.

Charles Spurgeon put it this way, "Once more, this man whom Christ saved at last was a man who could do no good works. If salvation had been by good works, he could not have been saved; for he was fastened hand and foot to the tree of doom. It was all over with him as to any act or deed of righteousness. He could say a good word or two, but that was all; he could perform no acts; and if his salvation had depended on an active life of usefulness, certainly he never could have been saved. He was a sinner also, who could not exhibit a long-enduring repentance for sin, for he had so short a time to live. He could not have experienced bitter convictions, lasting over months and years, for his time was measured by moments, and he was on the borders of the grave. His end was very near, and yet the Saviour could

27

save him, and did save him so perfectly, that the sun went not down till he was in paradise with Christ."[50]

Jesus then interacts with John and His mother Mary in John 19:26–27[51]: *Woman, behold your son. Behold your mother.* This is known as the word of relationship and teaches us just how important these relationships are in our lives. Kenneth O. Gangel has some interesting thoughts on these verses, "Most scholars understand this passage as a commitment of Mary, Jesus' mother, to John, since Joseph was probably already dead by this point and Jesus knew that none of his half-brothers had yet made a commitment to his mission. Perhaps at that point Mary might have remembered Simeon's prophecy: "This child is destined to cause the falling and rising of many in Israel, and to be a sign that will be spoken against, so that the thoughts of many hearts will be revealed. And a sword will pierce your own soul too" (Luke 2:34-35)."[52]

The next one is the only statement of Jesus on the cross found in two gospels. Matthew 27:46 & Mark 15:34 both record that Jesus said: *My God, My God, why have you forsaken me?*[53]

This is known as the word of abandonment. It is also the only thing that Jesus said that was stated in a different language in the Bible. Craig L. Blomberg said of Matthew 27:46 that, "The only "word" of Christ on the cross which Matthew records, chronologically perhaps the fourth of the seven, is the saying of v. 46. Perhaps because of the power and significance of Jesus' cry, the Aramaic was preserved and then given a translation."[54]

The English words ELI ELI (Strong's Concordance Number #G2241) in their literal meaning in the Greek language are "God, God." The meaning of the word LAMA (Strong's Concordance Number #G2982) is "Why." Lastly, the exact meaning of the word SABACHTHANI (Strong's Concordance Number #G4518) is "You have left (forsaken, abandoned) me."[55]

This phrase by Jesus is a quote taken from the book of Psalms, chapter 22[56].

1 My God, my God, why have you forsaken me? Why are you so far from saving me, so far from the words of my groaning? 2 O my God, I cry out by day, but you do not answer, by night, and am not silent. (NIV)

The next thing that Jesus chronologically states is found in John 19:28[57]: *I thirst.* This very simple statement is known as the word of distress.

Charles Spurgeon said in his sermon The Shortest of the Seven Cries delivered on April 14th, 1878[58] Jesus said, "I thirst," and this is the complaint of a man. Our Lord is the Maker of the ocean and the waters that are above the firmament: it is his hand that stays or opens the bottles of heaven, and sendeth rain upon the evil and upon the good. "The sea is his, and he made it," and all fountains and springs are of his digging. He poureth out the streams that run among the hills, the torrents which rush adown the mountains, and the flowing rivers which enrich the plains. One would have said, If he were thirsty he would not tell us, for all the clouds and rains would be glad to refresh his brow, and the brooks and streams would joyously flow at his feet. And yet, though he was Lord of all he had so fully taken upon himself the form of a servant and was so perfectly made in the likeness of sinful flesh, that he cried with fainting voice, "I thirst." How truly man he is; he is, indeed, "bone of our bone and flesh of our flesh," for he bears our infirmities.

After Jesus and God disconnect from one another for a brief period of time and after Jesus then displays His human discomfort of being thirsty Luke 23:46[59] offers us the word of reconciliation when Jesus says: *Father, into your hands I commit my spirit.* Of this verse Robert H. Steing states, ". Jesus, knowing that he had completed his departure/exodus (Luke 9:31), committed his spirit, i.e., his life, into his Father's hands in order to enter into his glory (24:26). In so doing Jesus is a model for his followers (cf. Acts 7:59)."[60]

Then finally we get the word of triumph in John 19:29[61]: *"It is finished."* And so it was, because Jesus became the propitiation for our sins. On these two verses Gerald L. Borchert said, "That word, Tetelestai (Greek), Consummatuum est (Latin), "It is finished" (English), has reverberated down through Christian history and theology as an expression of the finished work of Christ. As Paul and the Preacher of Hebrews stated, Jesus' death took place "once" for everyone (Rom 6:10; Heb 7:27; 9:12; 10:10). Moreover, the Johannine seer echoed this expression of the end of time when he wrote in his visions "It is done!" (Rev 16:17; 21:6)"[62]

In I John 4:10 out of the NKJV[63] it says this *"In this is love, not that we loved God, but that He loved us and sent His Son to be the propitiation for our sins."* And the word in the Greek is one of the few words that I believe is easier to say than in English. It is Hilasterion *hil-as-tay'-ree-on*[64] and it has a lot to do with a debt that has occurred.

So, I think the argument is pretty convincing, someone that can teach to the masses, preach through miracles, and preach while in misery is worthy of the moniker "Greatest Teacher of All Time." He was even better than my rapping wife.

CHAPTER THREE

Jesus is the greatest story teller of all time.

"The central Christian belief is that Christ's death has somehow put us right with God and given us a fresh start. Theories as to how it did this are another matter. A good many different theories have been held as to how it works; what all Christians are agreed on is that it does work."

– C.S. Lewis

I have a confession to make, I am not a fan of William Shakespeare. Honestly. I don't think I am alone on this topic. While the poetic, yet tragic ending of Romeo and Juliet and the poetic, yet tragic ending of Hamlet, and the poetic, yet tragic ending of Macbeth may be very popular . . . I am just not a fan.

Some consider Shakespeare to be the greatest storyteller of all time, Star Wars fans might actually disagree. George Lucas is a pretty good storyteller in his own right. The moment that we found out that Darth Vader was Luke's father was, well . . . downright Shakespearian.

We love a good storyteller; from Dr. Seuss to C.S. Lewis to J.K. Rowling to Walt Disney himself, the creative genius of a good storyteller can bring much success, fame, and fortune. I think we all know and appreciate a good story when we hear one, and a story can have a dramatic impact on our lives.

This is the reason I believe that Jesus used the art of storytelling to such the degree that He did.

I am going to argue in this chapter, that Jesus was not just a great storyteller, but that He was in fact, the greatest storyteller of all time. He utilized this talent to teach three important concepts to the audience of His day as well as to us now. The three concepts we are going to look at are Salvation, Forgiveness, and Grace.

One of the main ways Jesus accomplished this was through his unique telling of parables. Warren Weirsbe describes a parable as "a story that places one thing beside another for the purpose of teaching. It puts the known next to the unknown so that we may learn."

Francis J. Handy said "The word "parable" means literally "a placing beside," and in classical rhetoric it refers to juxtaposition, setting one thing by the side of another for the purpose of comparison and illustration"

There is a time in Scripture when Jesus was teaching not just one parable, but a set of parables together, with the theme Lost and Found, and He was teaching it primarily to the concept of salvation. The three parables are about the lost sheep, a lost coin, and a lost son.

We have a lost and found at our church, as most churches do. There have been some interesting things found in the lost and found. The typical church lost and found is stacked with Bibles, which leads you to wonder what the people are reading at home. I have found a lot of reading glasses. One time I found a single shoe, which led me to wonder if a one-legged man left it behind while church hopping.

If you Google strangest things found in a lost and found you will find two skulls, a human heart, $10,000, a vintage wedding dress and a rabbi costume . . . that must have been one wild Saturday night. However, when Jesus taught on lost and found, he had an entirely different approach to the topic.

The first story Jesus told was about a man who had a hundred sheep. One of his sheep strayed away from the flock and became lost. Every one of the man's sheep was important to him, so he left the ninety-nine and went to search for the one lost sheep. When he found it, he was so happy that he called all of his friends together and said, "Rejoice with me; I have found my lost sheep."

Then he continues this theme by talking about the lost coins in Luke 15:8-10.

> 8 "Or what woman, if she has ten silver coins and loses one coin, does not light a lamp and sweep the house and search carefully until she finds it? 9 "When she has found it, she calls together her friends and neighbors, saying, 'Rejoice with me, for I have found the coin which I had lost!' 10 "In the same way, I tell you, there is joy in the presence of the angels of God over one sinner who repents."

So the story is about a woman who had ten silver coins. Each of the coins was worth a day's wages. The woman counted her coins, "One, two, three, four, five, six, seven, eight, nine. Oh no! I have lost one of my coins," she cried. She turned on every light in the house, swept the floor, and searched until she found the one lost coin. When she found the lost coin, she called all of her friends and neighbors together and said, "Rejoice with me; I have found my lost coin."

Women of that day would often receive ten silver coins as a wedding gift. Besides their monetary value, these coins held sentimental value like that of a wedding ring; to lose one would be extremely distressing. The ten coins could have been this woman's life savings, meant to support her in a time of need. Upon discovering that one of the coins was missing, the woman would light a lamp in order to see into the dark corners, and sweep every part of the dirt-packed floor in hope of finding it. Although the woman still had nine coins, she would not rest until the tenth was retrieved. Her search was rewarded. Like the shepherd, she shared her joy with her friends and neighbors so they could rejoice with her.

So this woman has lost something that is equivalent to losing her wedding ring. So could you imagine now that someone lost their wedding ring and it was completely dark?

Matthew Henry suggests that "In the parable of the lost piece of silver, that which is lost, is one piece, of small value compared with the rest. Yet the woman seeks diligently till she finds it. This represents the various means and methods God makes use of to bring lost souls home to himself, and the

Saviour's joy on their return to him. How careful then should we be that our repentance is unto salvation!"

Jesus told these two stories to demonstrate God's love for us. We are God's children, but sometimes we get lost. When that happens, God doesn't give up on us. He searches for us and he won't stop until we are found. In fact, the Bible tells us that God sent his son, Jesus, to seek and save the lost. And just as the people in the story rejoiced when they found what was lost, Jesus said, "There is rejoicing in the presence of the angels of God over one sinner who repents."

The context of this story is going to fill in a few blanks as well. Jesus was talking to the Pharisees at the time, and the Pharisees were upset that Jesus was spending time with sinners. And not just that, but now all of the Pharisees are really upset that Jesus is dining with these people. However, if Jesus never dined with sinners, He would eat every meal alone.

The Pharisees were primarily not a political party but a society of scholars. They enjoyed a large popular following, and in the New Testament they appear as spokesmen for the majority of the population. About 100 BC a long struggle ensued as the Pharisees tried to democratize the Jewish religion and remove it from the control of the Temple priests. The Pharisees asserted that God could and should be worshipped even away from the Temple and outside Jerusalem. To the Pharisees, worship consisted not in bloody sacrifices—the practice of the Temple priests—but in prayer and in the study of God's law. Hence, the Pharisees fostered the synagogue as an institution of religious worship, outside and separate from the Temple. The synagogue may thus be considered a Pharasaic institution, since the Pharisees developed it, raised it to high eminence, and gave it a central place in Jewish religious life.

The thing about it is though that the Pharisees were sinners too. See, you were a sinner and Jesus looked all over to find you, and when He did, He rejoiced. And He rejoices when He finds any one of His children, whether they be religious sinners, or just regular old sinners.

So the question must be asked: If Jesus is so excited that one person gets saved as to compare it with a man finding his sheep or a bride finding her coins don't you think we should be equally excited to find those people who are lost?

You see if the coins in our parable represent us as His children, then who does the woman represent: God. And what happens when God finds one of His lost coins . . . The angels rejoice? No, we have been misquoting this for years, look at the verse again."In the same way, I tell you, there is rejoicing *in the presence* of the angels of God over one sinner who repents."

The rejoicing is in the presence of the angels of God, it's not the angels of God rejoicing. If the woman represents God, and the woman is so excited that she finds her gold coins that she runs to her neighbors to rejoice in the presence of her neighbors . . . God runs over to His angels every time someone gets saved and rejoices in their presence. How awesome is that? God once threw a party in your honor. Shouldn't we make an effort to find those who are lost so there can be a party for them too?

This should be one of our top priorities in life, to seek those whom are lost and to reunite them with their Creator. And this consequently is another point of the parable, that God did everything He could to make sure we were not lost. He sent His Son to offer redemption, and Jesus is alluding to this redemption shortly before it is manifested in the crucifixion and resurrection.

But there are a few other points to get from the first parable in Jesus line of three connected parables that is found in Matthew 18:12-14.

> 12 "What do you think? If any man has a hundred sheep, and one of them has gone astray, does he not leave the ninety-nine on the mountains and go and search for the one that is straying? 13 "If it turns out that he finds it, truly I say to you, he rejoices over it more than over the ninety-nine which have not gone astray. 14 "So it is not the will of your Father who is in heaven that one of these little ones perish.

There are a few points that we need to see from this parable. First of all, God intended us to stay in packs. That's why he calls us the body of Christ. You don't just one day decide that you're going to leave your arm at home do you? Of course not. Community is what we were intended for.

There is safety and comfort in a community. Church is intended to be a community. We are to stay together and to love one another equally. Isn't it interesting that in the wild, they have this whole concept of community down, and yet us as the church, the bride of Christ, made in the image of God, we struggle so much with it.

The second point is that there is real danger out there. The church is here for accountability, for support, and to keep you safe. Dolphins are one of God's most fascinating creatures, and they completely understand the idea of community. If one dolphin is sick or hurt, another dolphin will send out a distress call, and soon thereafter a school of dolphins are there surrounding their fallen comrade. They get underneath of him and lift him up to the surface periodically for air. And if a predator like a great white shark comes around, they will make a circle around the susceptible dolphin, at the risk of their own lives.

But now we come to our last point, and greatest point; and the point of the text that Jesus taught. You see, we are described in this parable as sheep, as a flock of sheep to be exact. Jesus says that if a shepherd has 100 sheep and 1 wanders off that he leaves the 99 behind to go find the one, and rejoices when he does.

This parable always confounded me when I was younger. Why would you worry about the one sheep that got away, why aren't you happy with 99. And then I had kids. It's not like if I drive to Disney with my kids and then realize that one didn't get back in the car, that I would say, "We lost Ethan. Oh well, we have another kid." No. I would turn over Heaven and Earth to find Ethan, because I love him and he is my child.

Ethan can always have confidence too, that if he is lost, his dad is definitely looking for him. If he knows that his dad will always be looking for him then he can have hope that soon he will be found. The only thing that is worse than being lost, is being lost with no one looking for you.

So here is the lesson Jesus would teach to us: It doesn't matter how crazy things get in your life. It doesn't matter how lonely life may seem. If Jesus says that He would leave the 99 to come find you, that means that He loves you individually, and personally, and there is nothing that can ever come in the way of that.

Then of course, comes the third in the line of three parables that Jesus teaches on salvation. The last one is the most famous of them all and it is the prodigal son. The prodigal son ran away, disgraced his father, spent all of his money and yet when he returned his dad came running to him.

This is how we know Jesus is the greatest storyteller of all time, because He paints a picture for us that we can know that no matter how far we get outside of God's will, it just takes one step to return to the Father and He will do the rest. How beautiful a picture to think of the Father running to meet his prodigal son that has returned.

The next lesson that He taught through His incredible storytelling ability was about forgiveness. And the story He taught on forgiveness may be one of His best ever. It is a parable that Jesus taught about a man that could not pay a debt and was released of the debt by a merciful man. It is found in Matthew 18:23-25:

> 23 "For this reason the kingdom of heaven may be compared to a king who wished to settle accounts with his slaves. 24 "When he had begun to settle them, one who owed him ten thousand talents was brought to him. 25 "But since he did not have the means to repay, his lord commanded him to be sold, along with his wife and children and all that he had, and repayment to be made. 26 "So the slave fell to the ground and prostrated himself before him, saying, 'Have patience with me and I will repay you everything.' 27 "And the lord of that slave felt compassion and released him and forgave him the debt.

In these verses Jesus told a story about one man who owed another man an extraordinary amount of money—"ten thousand talents" to be specific. That's a lot of money, millions of dollars in today's economy.

The day came when the debt was due, and the man was called in to account. The man couldn't pay and consequently was sentenced to "debtor's prison." There he would labor, together with his family, until the debt was paid off—even if it meant subsequent generations remained imprisoned.

The man, hopeless, threw himself on the ground and began to plead for mercy—more time to pay off the debt. Everyone watching this pathetic scene began to feel uncomfortable, because loan officers don't become successful by showing mercy. They're not called "loan bunnies" or "loan puppies"; they are called "loan sharks." If you don't pay, someone named Bruno shows up at your house to break your thumbs.

But then the most unexpected thing happened. This loan shark felt an emotion Jesus calls "splagma," a Greek word meaning a gut-level compassion for the guy. We don't know why. Perhaps he remembered his own children, or maybe he just identified with this guy—whatever—and his bottom lip started to quiver and a tear filled his eye. He then said the unthinkable: "Forget about it. You owe me nothing."

No one in the room could believe it, least of all the forgiven man. For the first time in his life, he felt free. He thanked the loan officer profusely and emerged from the courtroom a new man.

So what is Jesus trying to tell through this parable? Well, first of all, what is this all about? The Kingdom of Heaven. Who is the King? God. Who is the man who owes the debt? One of us.

If this truly represents the Kingdom of God, then God is the King, and we, as believers, are the ones who owe the debt. So according to this parable, what happens to the debt we owe? It is forgiven.

The old cliché goes; Jesus died a death we could not die to pay a debt we could not pay. And so how should we react after this debt is forgiven? We should be elated.

So is that the only thing we should get out of this parable, that God forgave our sins and we should be happy about that? Definitely not, because the context of this parable says we should get something completely different out of it.

Matthew chapter 18 starts out with Jesus trying to settle another disciple argument. They ask Him who will be the greatest in Heaven, hoping that He will mention one of their names, probably Peter, James, and John were spear-heading this campaign. What they didn't expect was that they were going to get a seventeen verse answer.

He basically said that in Heaven, the last shall be first and the first shall be last and those who are like little children will be the greatest in Heaven, and if you cause one of those people who are like little children to stumble, then woe to you, because it would be better for you to tie a heavy rock around your neck and jump off the Brooklyn Bridge than to cause someone to stumble. Oh and if it your eye causes you to stumble, cut it out, and if it is your hand that causes you to stumble, cut it off, because it is better to have one eye and go to Heaven then two eyes and go to hell. Oh, and back to my point, don't cause anyone to stumble because I came to seek and to save the lost. Yeah, yeah, it's like the shepherd/sheep thing, I will leave the 99 to find the one. Oh and if someone sins against you, here is what you do: You confront them and ask them to change their ways, if they do not, bring someone back with you and confront them again, and if they still won't change, take them to the Pastor and try again, and if they still won't change then that is all you can do because remember that whole rock around the neck/Brooklyn Bridge thing . . . that will be them now. But if you find a way to get along then I will give you what you ask for, because if two or more are gathered in my name, I will be there . . . (my paraphrase)

It almost seems as though Jesus forgot the question at one point. But leave it to Peter to break up the diatribe, he says 'Hang on, can you go back to the part about if someone wrongs you? How many times should I forgive them? Seven?'

You see the Pharisees believed that to be righteous means that if someone wrongs you the same way twice then you must forgive them twice, but the Rabbis believed that if someone wronged you the same three times you have to forgive them, but Peter made his number seven.

So after this long diatribe about anything and everything, Peter asks Him about forgiveness and he says to forgive people seventy times seven times and then tells the story we started out with about the man who was forgiven of his debt by a merciful king.

And so, if we were to sum up the parable we read in one word what would it be: forgive. And if we were to sum up what actions we should take as a result of the parable we read what would that action be: forgive. The message of the parable is simple: because we have been forgiven we should forgive others.

This parable reminds me of the Broadway play and movie Les Miserables. This play is an example of great storytelling. Jean Valjean was a bitter criminal who has just been paroled from a hard-labor camp in France. He stumbles alone late one night to the home of a priest, who invites him in and offers him food and shelter for the evening.

That night Valjean steals all the silverware in the priest's home. The priest, hearing some commotion in his house, gets up to investigate. Valjean punches him in the face and knocks him out. He then leaves with the stolen silver.

Early the next morning the police drag Valjean back to the home of the priest. The guard mockingly says to the priest, "He told us you gave this silver to him!" Being a paroled prisoner, all the priest has to do is confirm that Valjean stole the silverware, and Valjean will go back to prison—for life.

The priest, his face still hurt from the night before, looks at Valjean and says, "Why yes. Yes, I did. I'm very angry with you, Jean Valjean . . ." Then he adds, unexpectedly, '. . . because you forgot the candlesticks. Why did you forget the candlesticks? They are worth almost 2,000 francs."

The guard immediately orders Valjean to be released. Valjean, meanwhile, is dumbfounded at the turn of events. The priest knew he stole the silver, and Valjean knew the priest knew. And yet the priest not only vouched for the convict, he shoved additional wealth into his sack.

In explanation the priest says quietly to Valjean: "And now don't you forget it. Don't you ever forget it. You've promised to become a new man. "Jean Valjean, my brother, you no longer belong to evil. With this silver I've bought your soul. I've ransomed you from fear and hatred, and now I give you back to God."

Les Misérables is the story of how Valjean becomes "the new man" the priest declared he would become. The mercy of the priest transforms Valjean from a hardened criminal into a patient, kind, generous man who cares for the poor and the orphan. A recipient of great mercy, he becomes a giver of great mercy.

So that is the point of the parable: We have been shown great mercy by God, so we should show great mercy to others. We have been forgiven by God, so we should show forgiveness to others. We have been shown unmerited love and favor by God, we should show unmerited love and favor towards others.

So the man in the parable is a guy who owed a huge debt that he could never repay, and the law says that he should be thrown in prison until he can repay the debt, and his family will be forced to work in his place as slaves to pay this debt, but based on what the man owed and what a day's wages was for a slave or a servant in these circumstances, this was a death sentence for himself, his family, and several generations down the line if there is any. So when the king says that his debt is forgiven, he must have shown mercy, forgiveness, love and unmerited favor to all of the people that he came in contact with from then on.

This is where the plot twist comes. This is where Jesus goes from a great storyteller to the greatest storyteller of all time. The next part of this story is so shocking that the hearers definitely never would forget it. The conclusion is from Matthew 18:23-35:

> 23 "For this reason the kingdom of heaven may be compared to a king who wished to settle accounts with his slaves. 24 "When he had begun to settle them, one who owed him ten thousand talents was brought to him. 25 "But since he did not have the means to repay, his lord commanded him to be sold, along with his wife and children and all that he had, and repayment to be made. 26 "So the slave fell to the ground and prostrated himself before him, saying, 'Have patience with me and I will repay you everything.' 27 "And the lord of that slave felt compassion and released him and forgave him the debt. 28 "But that slave went out and found one of his fellow slaves who owed him a hundred denarii; and he seized him and began to choke him, saying, 'Pay back what you owe.' 29 "So his fellow slave fell to the ground and began to plead with him, saying, 'Have patience with me and I will repay you.' 30 "But he was unwilling and went and threw him in prison until he should pay back what was owed. 31 "So when his fellow slaves saw what had happened, they were deeply grieved and came and reported to their lord all that had happened. 32 "Then summoning him, his lord said to him, 'You wicked slave, I forgave you all that debt because you pleaded with me. 33 'Should you not also have had mercy on your fellow slave, in the same way that I had mercy on you?' 34 "And his lord, moved with anger, handed him over to the torturers until he should repay all that was owed him. 35 "My heavenly Father will also do the same to you, if each of you does not forgive his brother from your heart."

So here is a man that has been forgiven a huge debt that he could never repay of millions of dollars. He rushed home, feeling light as air, to tell his family the news of their release. As he crossed the street across from the courthouse, he saw an old colleague who owed him $3.

He grabbed the man by the neck and said, "Give me my $3." The guy said, "I'm sorry. I've had a bad week. I don't have any money. I'll pay you next week." "No!" the man shrieked. "If you can't pay now, you're going to prison."

I imagine that when Jesus was telling this story, at this point His hearers might have rolled their eyes. "Give me a break. Nobody forgiven of millions of dollars would throw someone in prison over $3." And that is Jesus' point exactly.

There is no way you could have any concept of what God has forgiven you of and be ungenerous in spirit toward others. If you are, it must mean you are unaware of the grace God has shown toward you. Someone saturated in the grace of the gospel develops an almost insane ability to forgive.

You see how the parable ends. The king sends the man who wouldn't forgive to prison because he wouldn't forgive his fellow servant. So what does the prison represent? No, not hell. He starts out by saying the Kingdom of Heaven is like, if someone is in the Kingdom of Heaven he is always in the Kingdom of Heaven.

The prison is a prison. Look, if you don't forgive someone who wrongs you, you know who suffers? You. The longer you hold your feelings of resentment toward someone inside, the longer you withhold mercy, forgiveness, love and unmerited favor, the longer your prison sentence becomes. Forgiving someone doesn't set that person free, it sets you free.

But the forgiveness that Jesus gave was permanent and all encompassing. It was this forgiveness that allowed us all to obtain redemption for our sins. This is the overarching theme of the parable.

To finish the idea that Jesus was the greatest storyteller of all time, let's look to the concept of grace. Grace was a key component of Jesus' teachings and main tenant of our Christian faith, so Jesus had to tell a really good story for this one. This story is found in Matthew 20:1-16.

1 "For the kingdom of heaven is like a landowner
who went out early in the morning to hire laborers for his

vineyard. 2 Now when he had agreed with the laborers for a denarius a day, he sent them into his vineyard. 3 And he went out about the third hour and saw others standing idle in the marketplace, 4 and said to them, 'You also go into the vineyard, and whatever is right I will give you.' So they went. 5 Again he went out about the sixth and the ninth hour, and did likewise. 6 And about the eleventh hour he went out and found others standing idle, and said to them, 'Why have you been standing here idle all day?' 7 They said to him, 'Because no one hired us.' He said to them, 'You also go into the vineyard, and whatever is right you will receive.' 8 So when evening had come, the owner of the vineyard said to his steward, 'Call the laborers and give them their wages, beginning with the last to the first.' 9 And when those came who were hired about the eleventh hour, they each received a denarius. 10 But when the first came, they supposed that they would receive more; and they likewise received each a denarius. 11 And when they had received it, they complained against the landowner, 12 saying, 'These last men have worked only one hour, and you made them equal to us who have borne the burden and the heat of the day.' 13 But he answered one of them and said, 'Friend, I am doing you no wrong. Did you not agree with me for a denarius? 14 Take what is yours and go your way. I wish to give to this last man the same as to you. 15 Is it not lawful for me to do what I wish with my own things? Or is your eye evil because I am good?' 16 So the last will be first, and the first last. For many are called, but few chosen."

In this parable, God is the owner, believers are the workers, and the vineyard is the Kingdom of Heaven. So let's look a little deeper now at what is the Kingdom of Heaven or the Kingdom of God?

I believe the Kingdom of heaven to be the sphere of salvation. The Kingdom of Heaven is the spiritual realm where those who are the children of God exist. The realm of salvation or the sphere of salvation is the sphere where God rules over the redeemed, where God rules through the grace of salvation.

The landowner went out early one morning to find some workers to whom he agreed to pay the worker a denarius. Now a dinereas was not normal day worker pay. It was better than that. It was a very fair wage. In fact, it was a very generous wage. It was standard pay for a skilled employee. It was standard pay for a Roman soldier. It was generally accepted as fair wages, not low, very generous. And both owners and workers agreed on this wage.

Now early they may have had some choice. In other words, they may have said, "Well, you know, there's some other men coming to hire men. And maybe we oughta wait and find out if somebody's gonna give us a better price, better wage." But this was good and they immediately signed up. The wage was attractive. And so he sent them into the vineyard at 6:00 a.m. to get to work.

Then the owner went out again at nine o'clock in the morning and hired more workers. They agreed to be paid whatever was right at the end of the day. He did the same thing at noon and again at five o'clock that evening. These last men were willing to work for that last hour, even though they would not earn much money.

"Again at mid-day, and yet once more at five o'clock in the afternoon he went out, and finding men on each occasion loitering about the market-place, he sent them also into the vineyard. In these cases, however, as was meet when the day was broken, the master did not promise any specific rate of wages; and the men, thankful for an opportunity of turning to some profitable account a day which would otherwise have been wholly lost, were content to accept whatever he might be pleased to give."

Now let's reread this passage and see what the Bible says would have happened next. "So when evening had come, the owner of the vineyard said to his steward, 'Call the laborers and give them their wages, beginning with the last to the first.' And when those came who were hired about the eleventh hour, they each received a denarius. But when the first came, they supposed that they would receive more; and they likewise received each a denarius."

So he pays those who started at 5:00. And then he pays those who began at 3:00. And then those who worked six hours, having begun at noon, and those who worked nine hours, having begun at 9:00. And the last batch who started at 6:00 are last. The more normal rule, which we like to live by, first come, first serve won't do. In fact, the whole thing becomes shocking in verse 9. "When those hired about the eleventh hour came, each one received a dinereas."

A dinereas a day is incredible. But a dinereas an hour, that's mind-boggling. A whole day's wage for one hour. And we can assume that he paid the ones that started at 3:00 the same thing and the ones who started at noon the same. And the ones who started at 9:00 the same. Generosity is wonderful. Now, the all day gang are starting to get excited. "What are we gonna get?"

And their curiosity kind of runs away with them and they begin to imagine that they're going to get more. In verse 10, "When those hired first came, they thought they would receive more. And they also received each one a dinereas." They had cherished, by the way, all through this process, they had cherished the silent expectation that when their turn came they would receive more because they'd worked longer. And when that didn't happen they could not contain their disappointment.

So verse 11 says, "When they received it, they - Greek word, egingoozoed. They egingoozoed. It's an onomatopoetic word. It means they mnmmmn - mumbled, grumbled. And they grumbled at the landowner saying, "These last men have worked only one hour and you have made them equal to us who have borne the burden in the scorching heat of the day." Literally, in the Greek, the burner of the day. I mean, this was a scorcher and we've been out there 12 hours. By the way, burner is often applied to the hot east wind that scorches the flesh, parches the lips and the throat. The evenings cool down, it's much like California.

One hour of work from 5:00 to 6:00 is nothing. It's absolutely insignificant compared to 12 hours through the burner of the day and the scorching, drying, irritating wind. How could they be equally paid? The reply is absolutely marvelous. But he answered, verse 13, and said to one of them, "Friend, etirus." Frankly, it's usually a rebuking term. Today we might say it this way. "Fellow - listen fellow. I am doing you no wrong. Did you not agree with me for a dinereas? Didn't we agree on this? Wasn't I faithful to what I promised you?"

Well, the answer of course is yes. Back to verse 2. "He had agreed with the laborers for a dinereas for the day." Verse 14. "Take what is yours and go your way. But I wish to give to this last man the same as to you." The only issue here was competitive jealousy, envy. They were still standing there holding the coin in their hand too stunned to leave and hoping that their pleading would get them more, that their murmuring would get them more.

When Jesus says, "Take what is yours and leave." Nothing's gonna change. In verse 15. "Is it not lawful for me to do what I wish with what is my own?" It's not illegal, is it? It's not unjust. It's not unfair, is it? Of course not. They received what was promised. They were paid in full by the one who had a right to give what he wanted and did give it. They hadn't worked all day. But listen to this. They hadn't worked all day, but had the same need. So he met that same need with his generosity.

Sometimes, we think the same way for so long that it is difficult to see things from a different perspective. That's also true of spiritual truths. Jesus was passionate about helping us understand that the Kingdom of God is different than we might expect. Jesus said that the Kingdom of God was near.

You see, a lot of Christians would be like the workers. We would be upset because we worked all day and other people only worked one hour. But if we just focused on ourselves and realized that we got paid an honest wage as previously agreed upon then there would be no problem. But it is the difference between having an earthly mindset and having one that is based in the Kingdom of God.

In this parable, Jesus pointed out that salvation is not earned, but given freely only because of God's great generosity, which goes far beyond our human ideas of what is fair. The message of the parable is that God's loving mercy accepts the lowest member of society on an equal footing with the elite. This parable may have been addressed in the presence of the religious leaders who "grumbled" because Jesus chose the "lowly" disciples and spent time with those considered unclean and sinful (Luke 15:1-2). Those who come to God—regardless of social strata, age, material wealth, or heritage, and no matter when in life they come—will all be accepted by him on an equal footing. Such generosity, such grace, ought to cause all believers great joy.

And then Jesus ends the story by giving this proverb: "So the last will be first, and the first last. For many are called, but few chosen." When you read the proverb, you say to yourself, "What does that mean?" And this proverb has baffled some Bible students through the years, and I think that's unnecessary. I think reading the parable explains the riddle with just some basic things to understand.

The first shall be last is sometimes referred to in the context of humility. Andrew Murray said in his book on the subject, ""The highest glory of the creature is in being only a vessel, to receive and enjoy and show forth the glory of God. It can do this only as it is willing to be nothing in itself, that God may be all. Water always fills first the lowest places. The lower, the emptier a man lies before God, the speedier and the fuller will be the inflow of the diving glory."

The way to understand this, like a couple of points in the Bible, is to think of it in terms of a race. Now the only way for the last to be first and the first to be last would be if they all crossed the finish line in the dead heat. Right? I mean, if you're last, you're last. But if you're last and first, and if you're first and last, that means you end in a dead heat. The only way to be first and last at the same time is to cross the finish line altogether. If there are ten people in a race and they're all first and they're all last, it's a tie.

It was so obvious. And that is the intent of the parable. It is to demonstrate one simple point. That everyone will finish equally. That God is no respecter of his own. That God treats all of his own equally. This proverb is very simple and very straightforward.

Well, what it's saying is that the last shall be first in the sense that those that came into the vineyard last to work and those that came in first to work will all receive the same reward. What is it talking about? It's not a teaching on economics. It's not a teaching on wages and employee benefits. It's a parable about the Kingdom. It's a parable about the spiritual dimension. It is not an allegory. It is a simple illustration made to make one spiritual point.

And what is that one spiritual point? The householder is God. The vineyard is the Kingdom. The laborers are believers in the Kingdom. The day of work is time. The evening is eternity when we receive our reward. The wage is eternal life. The steward is Jesus Christ who was given the task of rewarding His own.

The reversal noted in these words (and in 19:30) points out the differences between this life and life in the Kingdom. Many people we don't expect to see in the Kingdom will be there. The criminal who repented as he was dying (Luke 23:40-43) will be there, along with people who have believed and served God for many years. God offers his Kingdom to all kinds of people everywhere. God's grace accepts the world's outcasts. No one has a claim to position in the Kingdom; God will make the appointments—the last and first places cannot be earned, bought, or bargained for.

Hired laborers in ancient Israel were the lowest people on the social ladder, the lowest class of workers. They were basically unskilled. They were untrained and they were unemployed except for a day at a time. They were day laborers. Life for them frankly was somewhat desperate and precarious because they had to work in order to eat. If they didn't work, they didn't eat and neither did their families.

Slaves and servants had steady jobs. And even though they might have been somewhat poor, they could share in family benefits. The day laborers were never certain and even had to provide their own place to live. Because the pay was low, they lived in a bare subsistence level.

God gives all of us more than we deserve. You know the truth? The people that worked 12 hours didn't deserve a dinereas. It was very generous. The rest didn't deserve it either. So everybody's really in the same boat. Nobody deserved it. The people that worked one hour didn't deserve it. Neither did the people that worked 12. That's called grace.

One thing you need to know about the Kingdom of God is that it is upside down. For instance in our world we have worth based on our self, on success, on wealth. In the Kingdom of God, however everything is backward.

In Jesus' life we see what the Kingdom of God is like. All are welcomed, made whole, and forgiven. The blind see and the deaf hear; good news comes to the poor and justice comes to the wicked; prisoners are released. This is what the Kingdom of God is all about. And when He tells this story about the farmer and the workers, it is exactly what He is teaching about, the Kingdom of God. You see, the Kingdom is presently not a place with actual diameters. The Kingdom of God is all around us for those of us who believe. But one day we will be in Heaven where the Kingdom of God will have diameters and we will be shocked and amazed at who was in the Kingdom with us the whole time and we didn't know it.

As Shakespeare would put it: "O, wonder!
How many goodly creatures are there here!
How beauteous mankind is! O brave new world,
That has such people in't!"

CHAPTER FOUR

Jesus is the greatest hope of all time.

"Hope is one of the Theological virtues. This means that a continual looking forward to the eternal world is not (as some modern people think) a form of escapism or wishful thinking, but one of the things a Christian is meant to do"

– C.S.Lewis[65]

Hope is defined as a feeling of expectation and desire for a certain thing to happen or a feeling of trust.[66] Hope is a powerful thing and yet it is often misused in modern language and thus doesn't quite hold the same powerful meaning as is intended in Biblical literature.

For example, hope is such a flippantly used term that we can say, "I hope this person comes through for me." Or, "I hope someone actually buys this book." In this instance hope actually has a negative tone inserted into it. However, when hope is used in the sense Jesus teaches, it is used in an entirely positive way.

The Greek word for the word hope is the word "elpis" and it is defined as an expectation of hope or, in a more specific manner, joyful and confident expectation of eternal salvation. [67]

Elpis is a term familiar with the Greeks, because it is the name of a character in Greek mythology. Elpis was the personification and spirit of hope. In Hesoid's poem "Work and Days", Epimetheus opened Pandora's box against the advice of those around him. In doing so, Pandora's box was emptied of diseases and a myriad of other pains. The only thing remaining in Pandora's box was Elpis, or hope.

It was then written:

> "Only Hope was left within her unbreakable house,
> she remained under the lip of the jar, and did not
> fly away. Before [she could], Pandora replaced the
> lid of the jar. This was the will of aegis-bearing
> Zeus the Cloudgatherer."[68]

The implications for this mythological stories are many. However, it paints a picture that in every circumstance, when you have hope, things can be overcome. This was the message Jesus gave to the people who were hopeless.

Let me put it this way, I am a die-hard Tampa Bay Buccaneers fan. Every year before the season starts I will "hope" that the Bucs win the Super Bowl. Well, it's only happened once in out history and our chances have looked pretty bleak since then. But enter Tom Brady!

When the G.O.A.T. quarterback decides to come and play for your team, your hope level rises significantly. And so now when I "hope" that the Bucs win the Super Bowl it seems a lot more reasonable. However, this still isn't the Biblical definition of the term hope.

If hope (elpis) is described as a faithful expectation, and Jesus is the greatest hope of all-time, then things will be even more different than just a Hall of Fame quarterback renting a mansion in your city.

Let's suppose that we fast-forward in time and the Bucs do make it to the big game. They just have to win one more game and they are world champs. The greatest quarterback of all time has the ball in his hands in the fourth quarter and there is only 15 seconds left on the clock. Tom Brady's team, the Tampa Bay Buccaneers has a 24 point lead. Now I say that that I hope the Bucs win the Super Bowl . . . that is called elpis . . . a faithful expectation.

Anyone that knows football knows what Brady would do next. He would take a knee, hand the ball to the referee and end the game in what is known as the victory formation. Jesus is the greatest hope of all time because in Him we have our **victory**.

I think my buddy Paul describes it very nicely in Romans 8:37 "But in all these things we overwhelmingly conquer through Him who loved us." It says to me that God's desire is for us to live a victorious life.

Victory comes from the Greek word Nike and it means the winning of a battle, war, or any struggle, to conquer; to carry off the victory, come off victorious. If you've ever played on any sports team, and your team won the game, then you overcame your opponent, and you were victorious. In any kind of game or match that you've been in, be it a chess game, a tennis match, a video game, or a Boxing match, whatever it is that involves competition, and you came out on the winning side. Then, you had a Nike. You had a victory.

Well, what if you've never won anything. You've never won a door prize. Your name has never been called on the intercom when you were in school because you won this week's coloring contest. You've never won a card game. You've never won the family game of Charades. You've never won the 40 yard dash. You surely haven't won an argument with your spouse. You may have never won an argument with your dog. So you may not know how to get a victory.

In my experience a lot of Christians don't act like they are living a life of victory. In fact, they seem downright defeated. I will be honest and say that some times I do not feel as though my life is victorious. But the beauty of it is that Jesus is the greatest hope of all time, because even if you have never won anything on your own, you are victorious because you are on the winning team with Jesus.

Sometimes in life we get sidetracked and we forget about the things of God and all that He has done for us. God has a plan for each and every one of your lives. I wish I knew exactly what it was. I wish I could meet you, look you in the eye and say, God is going to grant you a beautiful family and a nice house and a successful law firm one day, but I cannot do that for you. God does not give us the entire road map for our lives, He gives us each step that we should take.

I wish sometimes that there was a map that showed my final destination and I think that I would be more inclined to follow God's steps but He doesn't do that. You see, God doesn't show us the finished masterpiece but He tells us each brushstroke.

Sometimes I know it may seem as though God really DOESN'T have a plan. Things are going badly in your life . . . your getting divorced, your girlfriend cheated on you, your best friend was the one she cheated with . . . sometimes it feels like God doesn't have a plan, but once you get a little bit further down the road of life you will be able to turn around and see where God brought you and see that God really DID have a plan. And you can have hope that His plan is always better than your own.

Jeremiah 29:11 says "For I know the plans I have for you," declares the LORD, "plans to prosper you and not to harm you, plans to give you hope and a future." We love this verse. We memorize it. We make posters of it with a random eagle in the background. What we sometimes forget is the context of that verse. God is promising a time of difficulty--70 years of exile. It is about that time of hardship that the Lord says "I know the plans I have for you.

God has a plan for each and every one of you. All He asks for you to do is follow Him. I wish sometimes that God would just show all of us what He desires for us. I wish He would just show us His plan. But if He did that we would not have any real and genuine faith. He shows us a step at a time,

God has made a promise to each and everyone of you. The promise is not that you will be filthy rich, the promise is not that you will finally get a date. The promise is found throughout the book of Deutoronomy and in the book of Hebrews when God says "He will never leave me nor forsake me."

This is it, this is the statement that you need to know. You need to know that no matter what you have done in your life, "God will never leave you or forsake you." No matter what you are going through "God will never leave you or forsake you." This should give you such confidence and such courage because you are NEVER alone, ever. This should fill you with more hope than Tom Brady leading your favorite team.

It is phenomenal to know that Jesus is our hope and He is our victory, but how does this get us through the rough days in life? How can we be victorious if it feels as though we are just barely surviving sometimes? The fact that Jesus is the greatest hope of all time doesn't just mean that He is our victory . . . He is also our **helmet.**

1 Thes. 5:5-8 puts it this way, "5 for you are all sons of light and sons of day. We are not of night nor of darkness; 6 so then let us not sleep as others do, but let us be alert and sober. 7 For those who sleep do their sleeping at night, and those who get drunk get drunk at night. 8 But since we are of the day, let us be sober, having put on the breastplate of faith and love, and as a helmet, the hope of salvation."

This passage says that we have the "hope" of salvation as a helmet. My family likes to ride bikes together. My wife is the concerned parent that always makes sure that the kids have all the protective equipment they need. They have elbow pads, knee pads, bubble wrap, bullet proof vest, and of course a helmet.

The helmet is the most important thing to have because if you don't have your knee pads and you fall you just get a scrape and maybe a cool scar. However, if you don't have your helmet on, something serious really could happen. It is the most important piece of safety equipment there is and that is what hope is described as, a helmet.

We could always go back to a football analogy here and talk about the need for helmets to be worn when 300 pound men are running full speed at a 180 pound running back. As tough as football players are, they never go onto the field without their helmets on. It protects them in the battle of the gridiron.

The problem with what I am saying though is that there were not bicycles around yet in Bible times. (I Googled it, they were invented in 1817) Football wasn't a thing yet either, so what could the Bible possibly be referring to when it says that the hope of salvation is like a helmet. In Bible days, a helmet was worn during an actual battle, an actual war.

Could you imagine young Jedediah going out for battle against the Philistine army and his mom makes him put on elbow pads, and knee pads, and bubble wrap, and a bullet proof vest, but he has no helmet on. The second the opposition saw him walking out into battle without a helmet on, he would be as good as dead.

The Bible describes the hope of salvation as a helmet because there is an actual war going within ourselves between good and evil, between the flesh and the Spirit. If you are wearing your helmet of hope you can know that no matter you go through in life, it is going to be okay because you have salvation and one day you will be with God in Heaven. Jesus provides us with this hope.

Jesus bringing this hope to life can be seen clearly through the impactful verse John 3:16. *"For God so loved the world, that He gave His only begotten Son, that whoever believes in Him shall not perish, but have eternal life.*[69]*"* John 3:16 has become the iconic verse of Christian culture. The verse has enormous power. The verse is so revealing. The verse is so straightforward. This is a verse of hope.

A.W. Tozer says in reference to this verse that. "Jesus Christ came not to condemn you but to save you, knowing your name, knowing all about you, knowing your weight right now, knowing your age, knowing what you do, knowing where you live, knowing what you ate for supper and what you will eat for breakfast, where you will sleep tonight, how much your clothing cost, who your parents were. He knows you individually as though there were not another person in the entire world. He died for you as certainly as if you had been the only lost one. He knows the worst about you and is the One who loves you the most."[70]

John 3:16 has become the iconic verse of our culture. For many decades people would go to sporting events holding up signs that say John 3:16 on them in the hopes that someone would see it and check it out. John 3:16 has been memorized by more people in more places than maybe any other verse. I wasn't saved and probably had never stepped foot in a church and I knew the verse John 3:16.

I am afraid to admit that John 3:16 doesn't have the same effect on me as it did when I first got saved. It is the law of diminishing returns. The more you hear something the less exciting it seems. But I think it is time we reexamine the verse and get reenergized by the magnitude of the verse that summarizes everything that we believe in and explains everything we live for. Because to understand John 3:16 fully and to grasp it, is to understand Jesus' purpose statement, let's look at John 3:16 in its context.

This verse is part of a conversation Jesus was having with a man named Nicodemus, which turned into a teaching moment. John 3:1[71] clearly identifies Nicodemus as being a Pharisee ruler of the Jews. The Pharisees were a group full of self-righteousness and most importantly they were against Jesus. The verse actually says that Nicodemus was a ruler of the

Jews and this is a little more specific. It means that he was a member of the Sanhedrin, a special counsel or courts of 70 people, and it was the highest Jewish assembly for government at the time of our Lord.

The members of the Sanhedrin make final decisions in legal disputes, judge the fitness of priests to serve in the temple, and decided on additions to the temple. So this man was pretty high up there and yielded a lot of power.

John MacArthur said in <u>The MacArthur New Testament Commentary</u>72 that "The Sanhedrin (from the Greek word sunedrion 'council') was the religious ruling body of the Jews in the Roman-occupied Israel. The Sanhedrin's authority was final in matters involving Jewish law, while its authority in civil matters was limited. Roman governors (such as Pilate, Felix, and Festus)and Roman-appointed rulers (such as the Herods) wielded the political clout in Israel."

But the thing that set Nicodemus aside from the rest of the Pharisees and even members of the Sanhedrin was that God was seriously working on his life. There are some that claim Nicodemus to be a coward; they thought the man was scared, because, in the three times that Nicodemus is mentioned in the book of John, the author makes a special point to let us know that he is the one who visited Jesus after dark.

His night visit indicates that John was showing that Nicodemus was afraid of being discovered as a follower or sympathizer with Christ. He would risk losing his prestige, power, and position if he were discovered. Nicodemus is often portrayed as a cowardly person. One commentary, for example, states that Nicodemus sought out "Jesus in 'the night' which has suggested to most of the interpreters that he was hesitant and afraid to be seen with Jesus, coming as he did in secrecy out of regard for his reputation and to protect himself."[73] Because the John discusses him as one who "came to Jesus by night" (John 7:50; 19:39)[74], his every action thereafter seems to be colored by the timing of this first visit.

There actually are some that side with Nicodemus. There are a few that believe that Nicodemus came to Jesus at night because he was a busy man. His official business as a ruler of the Jews might have kept Him so busy they had no other time to meet other than after business hours. Some also believe that Nicodemus feared the Jewish leaders so much that he had to meet Jesus secretly. He was risking a lot even to speak to Jesus privately.

The Jewish rulers hated Jesus and were plotting how they might kill Him, thereby ridding themselves of one who has become a thorn in their side. Jesus was widely popular among the common people, he performed miracles, he talked the force of divine authority, and he threatened their power over the people because he revealed their own hypocrisy. If they had known that Nicodemus was meeting with this vile enemy of the religious hierarchy, they would've turned on him and ruined him professionally and perhaps even physically.

So here we have this very prominent, powerful man approaching Jesus after dark. He starts this conversation by saying, "Teacher we all know that God has sent you to teach us. Your miraculous signs are evidence that God is with you."[75]

Nicodemus is complementing Jesus. He is doing what his colleagues would never do. He told Jesus that he was impressed by his teachings, he told Jesus that he was sent by God, and he told Jesus that his miracles were evidence of this. He didn't ask Jesus a question, Jesus gave Nicodemus an answer anyway.

Jesus knew what Nicodemus was there for, even if Nicodemus didn't know what he was there for. And Jesus says "I tell you the truth, unless you are born again, you cannot see the kingdom of God."[76]

Nicodemus was a very educated man. The members of the Sanhedrin generally were famous teachers of the Old Testament Scriptures and therefore highly revered. We can safely assume this to be the case with Nicodemus because Christ called him in verse 10 a respected Jewish teacher. Other translations say a master. He had mastered the Old Testament, he was very educated, and yet he was spiritually ignorant.

You see we know this because of his response. Nicodemus exclaimed, "What do you mean? How can an old man go back into his mother's womb and be born again?"[77] After Nicodemus asked this question about how to be born again Jesus said. "Except a man be born of water and Spirit he cannot enter into the kingdom of heaven."

This is what is known as the new birth. This is Jesus teaching about brining life to the dead. We know from Nicodemus's question that Jesus wasn't talking about a physical birth. When Jesus says we need to be born of water and the Spirit he's talking about two different births.

The first birth is our physical birth. That's the birth he's talking about when he says to be born of the water. And when he talks about being born of the Spirit that's when he's talking about our conversion experience.

Next Jesus places a verbal emphasis on this, some version will say "verily, verily" which means "truly truly" and is used to emphasize the importance of what is said. Twenty-five times in the book of John Jesus uses the double verily. And each of them is in connection with a great truth.

And we also see the importance of the new birth to Jesus because he says "except a man be born again". This is the only way you can enter the kingdom of heaven is to be born again. This is obviously very important to Jesus.

Jesus then appeals to the fact that Nicodemus would have known his Old Testament history really well. He says in John 3:14 that "Just as Moses lifted up the snake in the wilderness, so the Son of Man must be lifted up," This was a direct reference to Number 21:7-9, ". . . 7So the people came to Moses and said, "We have sinned, because we have spoken against the LORD and you; intercede with the LORD, that He may remove the serpents from us." And Moses interceded for the people. Then the LORD said to Moses, "Make a fiery serpent, and set it on a standard; and it shall come about, that everyone who is bitten, when he looks at it, he will live." And Moses made a bronze serpent and set it on the standard; and it came about, that if a serpent bit any man, when he looked to the bronze serpent, he lived."[78]

In this situation, we see the Israelites dying from serpent bites that God had sent because of their sinful ways. God said to make a serpent and as long as the people look to that serpent they will not die. So Jesus references that very story to illustrate in His teaching that He is here to bring death to life. As long as the sinful people look to Jesus they will not die.

Though Nicodemus still continues to question Jesus and Jesus continues to answer Nicodemus, Jesus goes on to say what we now refer to as John 3:16. You must wonder what would happen to a guy who heard those words spoken by Jesus Himself? There must be some change in his life. Well, what about Nicodemus? These words were as life-changing for Nicodemus as they have been for our world ever since.

A lot of times in the Bible we meet someone and I always wonder what happened to them. I want to know the follow up story. I love watching those

"Where are they now type shows." Well luckily for us Nicodemus' story doesn't just abruptly end.

In John 7 Nicodemus is back around the Pharisees again and they are trying to get Jesus. However, this time Nicodemus defends Jesus. He says in verse 51 of John 7, *"Does our law judge a man before it hears him and knows what he is doing?"*[79]

This verse shows that there was some sort of change in the man of Nicodemus. His cohorts were interested in the demise of Jesus, while Nicodemus was defending Him. This was a very risky thing to do, which shows His increasing courage and the change that has begun to occur within his heart.

John doesn't end the story of Nicodemus with just sticking up for Jesus. Jesus eventually was arrested, Jesus eventually was crucified, and Jesus eventually died. During all of this, His trusted disciples went into hiding. But Jesus needed a proper burial. So the Bible in John 19 says that Joseph of Arimethea went to ask for the body to prepare it for the tomb, and Nicodemus went with him.

The man who was so scared of his reputation that he met Jesus in the shadows; the man that was affiliated with the actual crucifixion of Jesus, the man who was searching for Jesus was the one who had the courage to go and prepare His body. This is because he heard the teachings of Jesus, and Jesus brought life to the dead soul of Nicodemus.

In our modern church vernacular: Nicodemus got saved! Nicodemus was changed from the inside out. And when you are changed by the Master you will NEVER be the same again. I said you will never be the same again. Nicodemus now had the helmet of hope that comes through salvation.

So I believe that Jesus is the greatest hope of all time because He is our **victory,** He is our **helmet,** and he is our **anchor.** Through the midst of life's storms, He is there and He is the fulfillment of every need that we have.

C.S. Lewis devoted an entire chapter to the idea of hope in his book Mere Christianity.[80] He argues that we all have longings and desires in life that we try to fill. However, everything in this world will eventually leave you feeling empty.

Lewis suggested that there are three different ways to deal with this dilemma. You can deal with it the fool's way, spending his entire life trying stuff that seems better and new, hoping to eventually fill his void with something of this earth. You can deal with it like the disillusioned, sensible man. This person ultimately decides that life is just supposed to be disappointing, and if you learn to lower your expectations for life, then you can trudge your way through it.

The final way to deal with the longings and desires that can't seem to be filled with things of this world is handle it the Christian way. "The Christian says, 'Creatures are not born with desires unless satisfaction for those desire exists. A baby feels hunger: well, there is such a thing as food. A duckling wants to swim: well, there is such a thing as water. Men feel sexual desire: well, there is such a thing as sex. If I find in myself a desire which no experience in this world can satisfy, the most probable explanation is that I was made for another world." This is what is understood to be hope. And this hope serves as an anchor in our lives to keep us steady.

Paul also addressed this topic of hope in his letters to the church. He wrote in Romans 5:5, "And hope does not disappoint us, because God has poured out his love into our hearts by the Holy Spirit, whom he has given us."[81] Therefore, hope is not a pie in the sky wish but is waiting with certainty on the day that God fulfills His promises.

Fortunately for us though, he goes on to state the good news of the one whose hope is in Jesus. "There is one man that is entitled to say: 'Tomorrow shall be as this day, and much more abundant.' Who is he? Only the man whose hope is in the Lord his God."[82]

This idea of hope may best be summed up by Edward Mote. It is he, in 1834, that wrote the lyrics to a hymn that says, "My hope is built on nothing less than Jesus' blood and righteousness."[83] The reality is that if your hope is built on anything else, then it truly becomes like sinking sand.

Nobody understood this idea any better than the apostle Paul. Paul was persecuted, arrested, and imprisoned on a number of occasions for his acceptance of salvation. When Paul was saved on the Damascus Road he had an instant change in his life. His story clearly describes what it is like for someone to go needing hope, to having hope, to using hope.

Paul wrote a majority of the New Testament and penned 2 Timothy while he was imprisoned and sentenced to death. Many ancient historians suggest that Paul was sentenced to beheading by the emperor Nero. According to ancient writings from people such as Tacitus, Suetonius, and Tertullian Nero was known as a being a persecutor of Christians. Bishop

Eusebius of Caesarea was the first to write that Paul was beheaded in Rome during the reign of Emperor Nero.[84]

According to his book <u>Ceasar and Christ</u>, Will Durant states, "Numbers only Christ Himself could count were put to death. Nero applied every ounce of his creativity to appoint means of death. Many were nailed to crosses. Others were covered with animal skins, tied down, and devoured by dogs. Still others were doused with flammable fluids and set on fire as torches in the night.[85]

Nero exercised such unimaginable cruelty toward Christians that many believed he must be the Antichrist. Peter lost his life in this terrible wave of persecution. But before he did he wrote 2 Timothy.

Paul wrote this as a letter and he wrote it to a guy named Timothy. Timothy was like his protégé, Paul would have been his mentor. And Paul wrote this letter to his young friend Timothy as the orders that Timothy should live his life by, these are very important directives. This is after all, the last known writings of a man that has accomplished so much for the Kingdom before he dies.

Paul starts out by giving a little introduction of who he is and reminding Timothy of who he is and where he came from. He talks about the faith of Timothy's mom and grandma and how influential they were in his life. He talks about the faith of Jesus, and how we should not be ashamed of it even if we are persecuted for it. And he gave a little update on some mutual friends that he and Timmy have together, and then we get to chapter 2.

2 You then, my son, be strong in the grace that is in Christ Jesus. 2 And the things you have heard me say in the presence of many witnesses entrust to reliable people who will also be qualified to teach others. 3 Join with me in suffering, like a good soldier of Christ Jesus. 4 No one serving as a soldier gets entangled in civilian affairs, but rather tries to please his commanding officer.[86]

As a manifesto to Timothy and consequently to followers of Christ everywhere in every time, Paul tells Timmy to be strengthened by Christ and to pass along his knowledge to others as well. And then we he says to join with me in suffering, like a good soldier of Christ Jesus. But considering the current situation that Paul finds himself in, this is tough.

Paul was nearly sixty years old and had taken a lot of beatings in his life. He was chained up and had an obvious lack of mobility because of this. It was probably cold and damp, Paul asked Timothy to being his cloak before winter. They tried to humiliate Paul by not letting him properly clean himself or dress in a respectable way. His bathroom and his bedroom would also be the same thing, causing hygiene issues as well as privacy issues. With all this being said, Paul still said that he was not ashamed of Jesus Christ and that we should share with him in suffering as a good soldier of Jesus Christ.

The greatest way that we know that Jesus brought the greatest hope of all time is because those people weren't scared to die because they would still be alive. In all of this, he told Timothy that he should continue to preach, to rebuke, to encourage, to study and to share everything that he knew about Jesus. Paul wanted more people to be brought from death to life even after Paul's physical body was gone.

So Paul writes what will be known as his final words in such a beautiful fashion: "6For I am already being poured out as a drink offering, and the time of my departure has come. 7I have fought the good fight, I have finished the course, I have kept the faith; 8in the future there is laid up for me the crown of righteousness, which the Lord, the righteous Judge, will award to me on that day; and not only to me, but also to all who have loved His appearing."[87]

Paul wasn't just pulling a word picture out of a hat. Anyone in the Roman Empire would know exactly what he was talking about. I wouldn't be the least surprised if these words spread and ultimately hastened his death.

According to Robert Graves in his book The Twelve Ceasers, "In A.D. 67, the year of Paul's death, Nero had the audacity to enter himself in the Olympic games. Mind you, Olympic athletes trained all their lives for the games. The thirty-year-old, soft-bellied emperor used medications to induce vomiting rather than exercise to control his weight. He was in pitiful shape and ill prepared, but who would dare tell him he could not compete?

He cast himself on a chariot at Olympia and drove a ten-horse team. "He fell from the chariot and had to be helped in again; but, though he failed to stay the course and retired before the finish, the judges nevertheless awarded him the prize."

Nero did not finish the race. Nevertheless, a wreath was placed on his head, and he was hailed the victor. He showed his gratitude for their cooperation in the ridiculous scam by exempting Greece from taxation.

For his processional entry into Rome he chose the chariot Augustus had used in his triumph in a former age, and he wore a Greek mande spangled with gold stars over a purple robe. The Olympic wreath was on his head. "Victims were sacrificed in his honour all along the route." You can be fairly certain they were Christians.

Needless to say, word of the humiliating victory spread fast. Soon after Nero returned to Rome, the apostle wrote his stirring final testimony: "I have fought the good fight, I have finished the race, I have kept the faith. Now there is in store for me the crown of righteousness, which the Lord, the righteous Judge, will award to me" (2 Tim. 4:7–8). The edict was signed for his execution. The apostle Paul desired one thing of his death. The same thing he desired in his life, to "have sufficient courage so that now as always Christ will be exalted in my body, whether by life or by death"[88]

What Paul had was hope. He had hope because of the victory Jesus had already won. He had hope because of the helmet of salvation that was protecting his mind. And He had hope because even in all his difficulties he had the unwavering certainty that He would join God in Heaven one day soon.

As a final discussion to Jesus being the greatest hope of all time because He is like an anchor, I would like to bring to your attention Hebrews 6:17-20. It says, "17 In the same way God, desiring even more to show to the heirs of the promise the unchangeableness of His purpose, interposed with an oath, 18 so that by two unchangeable things in which it is impossible for God to lie, we who have taken refuge would have strong encouragement to take hold of the hope set before us. 19 This hope we have as an anchor of the soul, a hope both sure and steadfast and one which enters within the veil, 20 where Jesus has entered as a forerunner for us, having become a high priest forever according to the order of Melchizedek."

I've thought a lot about this metaphor of Jesus being our anchor and it was never very satisfying to me. It is as though we are in a life boat and our anchor is just clinging to the dirt below us. Just because we have an anchor, it doesn't really make us any safer. And what is the rope just comes undone from the lifeboat, now it doesn't even matter that we own an anchor.

Then I read these verses in Hebrews again and I realized that my word picture is all wrong. The anchor isn't clinging in the dirt below us, it is firm and secure in the inner sanctuary. So a better word picture is that Jesus has gone to Heaven and attached His anchor to the cross. As we are in our life boat with hurricane force winds all around us, we see a rope fall from the sky. We grab onto the rope that is firmly anchored in Heaven.

But what if we are not strong enough to hold onto the rope during the toughest storms in life? We don't have to, because Jesus walks right out onto the water climbs in your boat takes that rope and ties it around his own waist. Then Jesus clings to you as you cling to Him. No one or no thing will separate the two of you, no matter how rough things get.

> My hope is built on nothing less
> Than Jesus' blood and righteousness
> When darkness veils his lovely face
> I rest on His unchanging grace
> In every high and stormy gale
> My anchor holds within the veil

CHAPTER FIVE

Jesus is the greatest Savior of all time.

"When Christ calls a man, he bids him come and die. It may be a death like that of the first disciple who had to leave home and work to follow him, or it may be a death like Luther's, who had to leave the monastery and go out into the world. But it is the same death every time—death in Jesus Christ, the death of the old man at his call. Jesus' summons to the rich young man was calling him to die, because only the man who is dead to his own will can follow Christ."

— Dietrich Bonhoeffer

I know what you are thinking. You know that in my opinion Michael Jordan is the greatest basketball player of all time and Tiger Woods is the greatest golfer of all time and Tom Brady is definitely the greatest quarterback of all time, but there is one great big, huge question . . . who do I think is the greatest tightrope walker of all time. The answer to that question is Nik Wallenda.

I don't know if you saw it or not, but I was watching with my family as Nik Wallenda walked across a volcano on a tightrope. I love this guy for a lot of reasons. Number one, he does stuff that I would never dream of doing. I get nervous watching him do it, there's no way I could actually do it. He has such a unique talent and I love the fact that God so clearly gives people unique talents. But most importantly, I love this because he is using his gifts and talents to glorify God every step of the way.

And as I watched with nervousness him walking across the tightrope with my family, I couldn't help but think how amazing a metaphor this is for our lives.

When Wallenda was out there on the tightrope he faced such unbelievable conditions. First of all, the path that he was walking on was extremely narrow. I don't know if you know it or not but the Bible says that wide is the path that leads to destruction but narrow is the path that leads to eternal life.

The elements were crazy. He trained in winds that were 90 mph to get ready for what he was going to experience on top of a volcano. The smell from the volcano was rotten, the gases were toxic and when that gas mixed with water (sweat) it became sulfuric acid.

And he is the first person ever to do it, so he was very much like Elsa in Frozen 2, he was walking "Into the Unknown." As he walked that tightrope for over 40 minutes commercial free on national television, he was singing praises to God. He was praying to his Father and he was telling the audience about how to overcome fear.

But the whole time, all I could think of is how God is our way maker. It stuck with me over and over again. No matter how difficult the circumstances are around you, that no matter how unknown the situation is that you are walking into, that each day . . . step by step by step, one foot in front of the other, HE WILL BE YOUR WAY MAKER.

This is the reason that I have entitled this chapter that Jesus is the greatest savior of all time, because He is the ONLY savior. This Savior, this Way Maker had a message for the disciples in John 14:1 and again in John 14:27 and it is a message that He was for all of you as faithful readers of this book.

Let not your hearts be troubled.

Let not your hearts be troubled.

Let not your hearts be troubled.

Not only is this important because He is our Way Maker and so we should not let our hearts be troubled. Not only is this important because He is our Savior and so we should not let our hearts be troubled. There is more to this phrase when you look at the context of when He said this, and the person that He said it to, Peter.

You see, in order for Jesus to be our Way Maker you have to let Him show you the way. Peter thought that he knew the way all by himself. Peter said that he could handle anything. Peter said that he would lay down his life for Jesus. And can you imagine how Peter's world was rocked when Jesus told Peter that he would actually deny Him 3 times?

So, if you want to be truly led by the way maker you must be like Peter in this instance, he said that he already knew the way. One of the biggest things that stands between you and God being your way maker is your pride.

My best friend growing up was guy named Big Greg. He wasn't really that big, but there was another Greg in the youth group so the Youth Pastor started calling him Big Greg and 20 years later I still call him that. When we started driving we both had pretty bad cars and the GPS wasn't out yet.

I remember one day that we had two cars full of people going to our friend Edwin's house. Big Greg had never been to Edwin's house and didn't even know his name. We stopped on the road and Big Greg asked me what his name was and I told him, Big Greg then said that he knew the way.

To this day we have no idea what Big Greg was thinking, but I bring it up every chance I get to make fun of him. Even though he had never been to Edwin's house before, he thought he knew the way. This is exactly as it was with Peter.

Peter had no idea what was about to happen in the life of Jesus, but Peter thought that he definitely knew the way. And this is what Peter was telling Jesus. But don't you love that the very next thing after Jesus told Peter that he would deny him 3 times is that He said . . . Let not your hearts be troubled.

I wonder what He was referring to. Maybe, He was telling the disciples that even though one of them would turn their back on Him that everything would still be okay.

Maybe He is understanding that the disciples realized things would never be the same again. This is such a huge part of life. People die, pastors move on, the friendships you had that were once strong drift away and throughout all of it . . . Let not your hearts be troubled.

Now that you know the context, check out the Scripture in John 14:1-9

"Do not let your hearts be troubled. You believe in God; believe also in me. 2 My Father's house has many rooms; if that were not so, would I have told you that I am going there to prepare a place for you? 3 And if I go and prepare a place for you, I will come back and take you to be with me that you also may be where I am. 4 You know the way to the place where I am going." 5 Thomas said to him, "Lord, we don't know where you are going, so how can we know the way?" 6 Jesus answered, "I am the way and the truth and the life. No one comes to the Father except through me. 7 If you really know me, you will know my Father as well. From now on, you do know him and have seen him." 8 Philip said, "Lord, show us the Father and that will be enough for us." 9 Jesus answered: "Don't you know me, Philip, even after I have been among you such a long time? Anyone who has seen me has seen the Father. How can you say, 'Show us the Father'?

Jesus said He prepares a place for us. This means that it doesn't matter how bad things get in life that one day we will make it to the other side and it will be beautiful. And in this place there will be no Covid 19, Covid 20, Covid 90210, no murder, no cancer, no racism, and let me tell you there will be one table. There won't be tables for all the different races and nationalities; there will be one table where together all of us that love Jesus will be together and break bread together and collectively sing Holy Holy Holy is the Lord God almighty who was and is and is to come . . . so we better get used to each other, because we might just be spending an eternity together.

Jesus is said to be the bridegroom while we (the church) are the bride. In those times the bridegroom would propose and then they would go away for around a year and prepare a house for them to live in. Our bridegroom was a carpenter here on Earth and now the master carpenter said He is not just going to build us a house, He is going to build us a mansion so we better get ready because one day soon the bridegroom is coming back for us. And we need to have faith that this is exactly what is going to happen, and Jesus says that we all know the way in which this will happen.

Let me jump back over to Nik Wallenda again. Did you know that when he walked across the volcano in Nicaragua that the inside of the volcano that he walked across was nicknamed the mouth of hell? And did you know that the volcano was actually named Massaya which sounds an awful lot like Messiah to me. Jesus is our Messiah and He is the way and He will be your Messiah and He will get you over the mouth of hell and He will get to the other side.

And now leave it Thomas to ask the next question and be the buzzkill. "How can we know the way?" If you want to allow God to be your way maker, you must trust that He is just that and you must replace all of your doubts with faith and confidence and He will make the way.

I just have to say that my wife is amazing and wonderful . . . but . . . there is one thing that she has always done that I just don't understand. She has always argued with the GPS. She has doubted time and time again that the GPS know the right way to go.

This will be difficult for some of you. This will be a constant life struggle for some of you. But you must have confidence not that Jesus knows the right way to go, but that HE IS THE WAY. He says I am the way the truth and the life. You must believe that He is the truth and that He is the only way to eternal life. There is no shortcut, there is back way, there is no waiting until the traffic dies down. There is Jesus. Jesus. Jesus. He is the WAY!

We started by hearing from Peter who was prideful and thought that he knew the way, then we go to Thomas and he was doubtful that Jesus was the right way and next we hear from Phillip. And if I had to say which one these three disciples responses to Jesus being the way is most like people that are a part of the American church, I choose Phillip.

When Phillip was first called to be a disciple he was the "come and see" disciple. He followed Jesus, went and got his buddy Nathaniel and when Nate started asking questions, Phillip said come and see.

But a lot has changed since that time. I think the same goes for a lot of us. I know Jesus because my neighbor Mrs. Gant knocked on my door when I was 12 years old and said she would drive me to church if I wanted to go, she said come and see. After I got saved and fell deeply in love with Jesus, I would wait at her garage door every Sunday morning for the beautiful sound of her garage door opening because I knew that meant it was time for church.

But then life hits, but then struggles occur, but then things get difficult, and we get jaded. Now the way the typical American church operates is that the congregation spends more time complaining about their church than they do inviting people to it. We go from inviting people to church and saying "come and see" to be jaded about church and saying "how can I see?" And now we see that Phillip has changed from the "come and see" disciple to the "how can I see" disciple.

If you want God to truly be your way maker you must not be confused, you must not get stuck trying to figure out every detail and just trust that Jesus is the way, and you MUST STOP TRYING TO MAKE EVERYTHING ABOUT YOU!

You see Phillip says Jesus can we just see the Father . . . if we see the Father then I will start being who God made me to be. Jesus saw right through that question . . . the more I read this question and the more I read Phillip's response the more I see that Phillip wasn't confused, he was making excuses.

And this is exactly where the state of the American church is right now. If we asked you why you are not living for God right now you would have lot of excuses . . . things are hard, I have to stay focused on my work, that person hurt me, Christians are hypocrites, I just like things the way they were . . . you have a bunch of excuses. Well things just aren't the same now in church as they were before, that Pastor wears jeans, well everyone is always arguing . . . excuses, excuse, excuses.

Phillip said if I could just see the father then I would know . . . excuses, excuses, excuses. I'm here to tell right now that God is calling you to stop being an excuse maker so that He can be the way maker in your life. I said God is calling you to stop being an excuse maker so that He can be the way maker.

When Nik was about to walk across the volcano, he could have made a lot of excuses. It's too hard, the winds are too heavy, there's sulfuric acid in my eyes. But did you know that he had a whole lot more baggage that he was carrying than just that. He lost family members to the tightrope, he had seen his sister fall just months before and break every bone in her face. He knew he had to keep going, he knew he had to overcome his fear, he knew he had to let God be his way maker.

What excuses are you making right now that is preventing God from being your way maker? Because ultimately, when we are talking about Jesus being the Way Maker, about Him being the greatest Savior of all time, even more so than walking across a tightrope on top of a volcano, it is a matter of life and death. The concept of going from death to life can be seen clearly in Paul's letter to the church of Ephesus.

Ephesians 2:1-3 says "1 And you were dead in your trespasses and sins, 2 in which you formerly walked according to the course of this world, according to the prince of the power of the air, of the spirit that is now working in the sons of disobedience. 3 Among them we too all formerly lived in the lusts of our flesh, indulging the desires of the flesh and of the mind, and were by nature children of wrath, even as the rest."

Paul begins the second chapter of Ephesians by showing the sharp contrast between those who are lost and those who are saved. He begins by describing the lost person. He does this through reminding the believers in Ephesus of what they were like before they followed Jesus.

He says first that lost people are dead. They are not just sick, but they are dead. This is a truth that comes all the way from the book of Genesis, when sin entered the world. So in essence, right now on Earth we are living in a graveyard.

He then says that lost people follow the world's kingdom and the world's ruler, which is Satan. Satan is not omnipresent, but he does have a demonic army that does his bidding and he is in control of a lot of leadership of this Earth, which means those who are not following Christ are following the Enemy. Because of this, they live in oblivious disobedience to the things of God.

Paul then reminds us that we were all that way at one time. It is certainly true that some people got more involved in the ways of the world than others before they accepted Christ, but that is an irrelevant point. A "moral" lost person is still dead and disobedient. And we all are deserving of the wrath of God without accepting His Son as our savior.

Ephesians 2:4-7 says "4 But God, being rich in mercy, because of His great love with which He loved us, 5 even when we were dead in our transgressions, made us alive together with Christ (by grace you have been saved), 6 and raised us up with Him, and seated us with Him in the heavenly places in Christ Jesus, 7 so that in the ages to come He might show the surpassing riches of His grace in kindness toward us in Christ Jesus."

Then there is a dramatic and abrupt switch to his topic in verse 4 when he starts out by saying, "But, because of His great love for us, God . . ." No more beautiful words could have been written and Paul shows that he is about to unpack the good news after discussing the bad news first.

He says that because of the mercy and grace of God, because of His great love for us, He made us alive when were dead. When we were deserving of death and punishment, He gave us life and reward. And He is going to sitting us in the heavenly realms one day as an expression of His grace.

Ephesians 2:8-10 says "8 For by grace you have been saved through faith; and that not of yourselves, it is the gift of God; 9 not as a result of works, so that no one may boast. 10 For we are His workmanship, created in Christ Jesus for good works, which God prepared beforehand so that we would walk in them."

After this Paul gives a couple of verses that have been memorized and recited for centuries that has within it amazing doctrinal truth and enough revelation for someone to accept Christ's free gift of eternal life with just these verses. Paul begins my pointing out life without Christ, he then describes the grace and mercy of God, He then tells us that we had absolutely nothing to do with earning this amazing gift, and he tells us in verse 10 that we are God's handiwork.

Verse 10 is one of the most encouraging verses in the Bible. The word handiwork is translated poema (GK4160) and it is obviously where we get our word poem. To think that we are God's handiwork, his masterpiece, his poem, is unfathomable. And He has great works for us to do here in Earth, which means He has a plan for all of our lives, we are not an accident, we are His poem.

Matthew Henry in his commentary on this chapter of the Bible starts by pointing out the stark reality of our spiritual condition without Jesus. "Sin is the death of the soul. A man dead in trespasses and sins has no desire for spiritual pleasures. When we look upon a corpse, it gives an awful feeling. A never-dying spirit is now fled, and has left nothing but the ruins of a man. But if we viewed things aright, we should be far more affected by the thought of a dead soul, a lost, fallen spirit."

However, just as this chapter starts out somber and turns victorious, so too does his commentary. "The goodness of God in converting and saving sinners heretofore, encourages others in after-time, to hope in his grace and mercy. Our faith, our conversion, and our eternal salvation, are not of works, lest any man should boast."

The Old Testament prophesied that this would be the case in the book Ezekiel. Ezekiel was a prophet of God. Back in the day, this was the primary way God talked to people. We know He started out by actually showing Himself to people in different ways. When Jesus was here, He spoke through Jesus because He was Jesus. And now He has sent His Spirit to dwell inside of us and He speaks through His Spirit, because He is the spirit, and He speaks through His word, and He speaks through His people. But for a time called the prophetic age, He spoke through these prophets.

I wonder what it would have been like to be a prophet. In one sense, God was speaking directly to you so people would have wanted to be around you to hear from God. On the other hand, not all prophets had very positive messages from God and so you may not have been invited to a lot of parties.

Ezekiel seemed to be a guy who had to give rather unpopular messages to God's people. In fact, in preparation for his time as a prophet to the people of Israel, he was made to eat a scroll that had on it what he was supposed to say to the Israelites and it was described in the Bible as a scroll of lamentation, mourning, and woe . . . yeah, this guy was going to be real popular.

Also in his preparation, he was given a very specific diet and very specific instructions of what to do. He was supposed to lay on his left side for 390 days to represent one day for every year that of rebellion charged against the house of Israel. Then he was supposed to flip over to his right side and do it again for 40 more days to represent one day for each year of rebellion for the house of Judah.

He was told to shave his head, which was a sign of humiliation and he was told the exact amount of water to drink and how to make the bread he was supposed to eat, and how this bread was to be cooked on human excrement.

That's when Ezekiel said, "whoa, whoa, whoa." And so God allowed him to cook it using cow excrement instead . . . a lot better.

But of all the things God told Ezekiel, none of this is what I would have had the hardest time with. The part that I would have the hardest time with is that God tells him that he is going to go through all this preparation, and deliver a very unpopular message, and . . . they won't listen to you.

I can't even imagine what that must have been like for him. All of this preparation and the people weren't going to listen. It would be like God tells me to write this book and I spend years laboring on it, but God tells me that no one will read it . . . but write it anyway.

But as I do a lot of times when I think about the people of Israel, I realize just how much their plight resembles ours. How many times have we heard directly from God about what we are to do and we don't do it? How many times have you been given a message from your Pastor and you have ignored it? How many times have you purposely done what you know you are not supposed to do or have not done what you are supposed to do?

I am willing to bet a lot. And, to be honest, I have done it a lot myself. So when God goes out of His way to describe just how rebellious and stubborn the nation of Israel is, I think we could all agree that He just as easily could be describing us.

So with that being said let's take a journey to a place where God was revealing to Ezekiel a very familiar vision, and try to put yourself there. And let's figure out together how this specific vision given to Ezekiel long after his time of preparation applies to us today.

So Ezekiel is there and he sees a vision that is described as a valley of dry bones. Let's think about this phrase for a minute.

Valley: whenever a valley is mentioned in the Bible it refers to a dark, low place. Mountaintop equals good, valley equals low. And so, being that they are in a valley, this is a dark, low place.

Bones: Well, unless someone just got done tearing up a bucket of chicken, bones are usually not a good thing, either. Lying all around Ezekiel are bones of dead people. And just to make sure we know that they have been this way for a while he uses the word dry to describe these bones. These bones have been dead for a long time.

And so then God asks Ezekiel a question, leading him. He asks, "Can I make these bones come to life?" Now Ezekiel was a very wise man. He did not answer the God of the Universe with an answer that would put him on the same level as God. He answered this way:

"O sovereign Lord, you alone know."

I remember very clearly the day I asked my wife to marry me. I planned it all out. It all had meaning and was supposed to be very heart-felt and personal. And spoiler alert: She said yes.

But later that night I remember her getting a very thick binder full of papers and magazine articles, all with labeled dividers in it and plopping it down telling me that it was her wedding notebook. So after recovering from the initial shock of how detailed she was already, I decided to roll up my sleeves and get involved.

So she comes to me and says, "what do you think about these flowers?" I said, "I don't know if I like them. What else were you thinking of?" Well that wasn't the right response. I was young and foolish.

I got some wise counseling and prayed long and hard about those flowers. And the next time she asked me my opinion on something about the wedding, I replied,

"Oh Sovereign wife, only you know."

God didn't really didn't want Ezekiel to answer, He wanted to tell him. Ezekiel was a lot wiser than me. And the answer was a resounding, "Yes!" Of course God can do that.

So then as though this wasn't weird enough that he is standing in the middle of the valley of dry bones, God gives him a bit of a strange request. God tells Ezekiel to prophesy to these bones.

Now this is a little weird, and I may have questioned God a bit, but nowhere in Scripture does it indicate that Ezekiel questioned God. Because you see, in his preparation for being a prophet Ezekiel had an encounter with God, and when you have a true encounter with God, you are forever changed. And so he did it.

God told him basically to preach to these dry bones. And when you preach to them, preach to them with the Spirit. The actual word is the word "rhooa, and Ezekiel did it without question.

The word rhooa is a word that we find very early on in Scripture. That word Spirit is the same word breath that is used here. God is asking Ezekiel to preach the very breath of God or the very Spirit of God into these bones, and that is what he did. And then there was a loud sound.

Can you imagine what it must have been like to be there and to see all of those bones start rattling. And then it says that tendons began to form together and bones were connecting to bones.

Talk about a scary moment. I think I may have been alright during this part. But then skin was put on them, and eyeballs, and noses, and ears. It is like me and Baby Kate and Ethan putting together Mr. Potato Heads. God was just forming all of these bones and turning them into recognizable people.

And I think the scariest part would be when they sat up. I can just imagine they all get eyes and ears and a mouth and skin and they all sit up and their eyes are fixed on the person standing in the middle of the valley. If I were Ezekiel, this is where I would be running.

But then in verse 9 God tells Ezekiel to keep going, and He did and then the rhooa entered them. And then the breath of God entered them, and then the Spirit of the Lord entered them and they stood up.

This is what is so interesting. You see, before they had the breath of God, they looked just like any other human would. You wouldn't be able to tell any difference between them and anybody else . . . and yet they are dead.

If we had to use our modern-day vernacular to describe them we would probably call them zombies. They are people in the flesh, they look just like anybody else, except they are dead. But God breathes life into them and they stand and when they stood the Bible describes them in verse 10 as a vast army.

Let me relate this story to us now. I believe we are living in the valley of dry bones. We work in the valley of dry bones, we go shopping in the valley of dry bones, we have family members in the valley of dry bones, and we are surrounded with people who look just like we do, but they are actually dead.

When the Bible describes people that are lost, it never mixes words. It doesn't say that some people are good and some are bad, it says that some people are dead and some people are alive.

And we are surrounded every day of our lives with people who are dead, but they may think they are alive, and you may think that they are alive . . . but they have never had the breath of God breathed into their lives, they have never had the Spirit of God enter their lives, they have never experienced the rhooa. And it is our jobs, just like Ezekiel to prophesy the breath into their lives, to tell them about the Spirit of God.

If you are a believer, if you are a Jesus follower, if you are a Christian . . . you have had the very breath of God breathed into your life and when the breath of God enters your life, you stand! And when you stand, you will be led by the greatest Savior of all time and He will continue to make the way.

However, if we are going to talking about Jesus be the greatest Savior of all time and how He makes the way and how He brings death to life, this book cannot end until we mention the story of Lazarus. The story of Lazarus also parallels to the story of Ezekiel.

John 11:38-44 "38 So Jesus, again being deeply moved within *, came to the tomb. Now it was a cave, and a stone was lying against it. 39 Jesus said, "Remove the stone." Martha, the sister of the deceased, said to Him, "Lord, by this time there will be a stench, for he has been dead four days." 40 Jesus said to her, "Did I not say to you that if you believe, you will see the glory of God?" 41 So they removed the stone. Then Jesus raised His eyes, and said, "Father, I thank You that You have heard Me. 42 "I knew that You always hear Me; but because of the people standing around I said it, so that they may believe that You sent Me." 43 When He had said these things, He cried out with a loud voice, "Lazarus, come forth." 44 The man who had died came forth, bound hand and foot with wrappings, and his face was wrapped around with a cloth. Jesus said to them, "Unbind him, and let him go."

Ezekiel is referred to as the son of man. Jesus was referred to as the son of man. Ezekiel was to deliver a message of eventual salvation to people that wouldn't listen. Jesus was to deliver a message of eventual salvation to people that wouldn't listen. Ezekiel was in an actual valley. Jesus was in a spiritual valley. Ezekiel was told to prophesy to dead bones. Jesus spoke to a dead body. When Ezekiel spoke to bones stood up. When Jesus spoke Lazarus stood up.

Matthew Henry says in reference to Lazarus that "The death of Lazarus was in a peculiar sense a sleep, as that of Jairus's daughter, because he was to be raised again speedily; and, since we are sure to rise again at last, why should that make any great difference? And why should not the believing hope of that resurrection to eternal life make it as easy to us to put off the body and die as it is to put off our clothes and go to sleep?" So the third parallel then becomes that just as the dry bones were dead and came to life, and just as Lazarus was dead and came to life, so too does the new believer enter from death to life.

What Jesus offers to us as believers in Christ is what is referred to as redemption. Redemption is defined as the action of saving or being saved from sin, error, or evil. Jonathan Edwards said, "The work of redemption and the work of salvation are the same thing. What is sometimes in Scripture called God's saving his people, is in other places called his redeeming them. So Christ is called both the Saviour and the Redeemer of his people."

Paul writes about this concept of redemption when he wrote Romans. "I consider that our present sufferings are not worth comparing with the glory that will be revealed in us. For the creation waits in eager expectation for the children of God to be revealed. For the creation was subjected to frustration, not by its own choice, but by the will of the one who subjected it, in hope that the creation itself will be liberated from its bondage to decay and brought into the freedom and glory of the children of God. We know that the whole creation has been groaning as in the pains of childbirth right up to the present time. Not only so, but we ourselves, who have the firstfruits of the Spirit, groan inwardly as we wait eagerly for our adoption to sonship, the redemption of our bodies."

Joseph Benson said of this verse, "From dust and death to glory and immortality, when our heavenly Father shall bring us forth before the eyes of the whole world, habited and adorned as becomes his children. Persons who had been privately adopted among the Romans, were often brought forth into the forum, and there publicly owned as the sons of those who had adopted them. So at the general resurrection, when the body itself is redeemed from death, the sons of God shall be publicly owned by him in the great assembly of men and angels."

Matthew Poole comments on it that, "But why of our body, and not of our souls? Because their souls would be in actual possession of the inheritance before that day, or because the miseries and troubles of this life are conveyed to the whole man by the body, so that the redemption of the body is in effect the redemption of the whole man."

Eugene Nida of the American Bible Society told about the translators' search for a word of phrase in a West African language to translate "redemption" or "salvation." Finally, they came upon a fitting image . . .

In that people's past, tribes would fight each other, take prisoners, and march them to a city on the coast where they were to be sold to the slave traders. If a relative or friend among the slaves were recognized, he could be bought for a price. The redeemed slave would then have the iron collar removed from his neck. In the tribe's native language, the process was described as "taking his head out" in order to set him free.

In the Bible of that language, then, "redemption" would come to be translated as "taking his head out"—a fitting image for the last-minute rescue which Christ has made by buying freedom at a price.

The act of Jesus being the redemption for us all didn't begin in the New Testament however, it began at the beginning of Creation. God first allude to this redemption in Genesis 3:15, which is known as the protoevangelium or "first gospel". In this verse God is talking to Satan, through the serpent, as to what his punishment shall be. He says, "And I will put enmity between you and the woman, and between your seed and her seed; He shall bruise (or crush) you on the head, and you shall bruise him on the heel."

God being the first one to tell of the gospel says that while Satan may get to bruise the heel of Jesus, Jesus will crush the skull of Satan, thus foretelling, thousands of years prior, of the great redemption story of Christ.

John Calvin says of these verses that, "I therefore conclude, that God here chiefly assails Satan under the name of the serpent, and hurls against him the lightning of his judgment. This he does for a twofold reason: first, that men may learn to beware of Satan as of a most deadly enemy; then, that they may contend against him with the assured confidence of victory."

From the garden we can move ahead and see Noah as a type of Christ. When the world was about to be destroyed by flood God told him to build an ark to preserve humanity. God's directive is recorded in Genesis 7, "Then the Lord said to Noah, "Enter the ark, you and all your household, for you alone I have seen to be righteous before Me in this time. You shall take with you of every clean animal by sevens, a male and his female; and of the animals that are not clean two, a male and his female; also of the birds of the sky, by sevens, male and female, to keep offspring alive on the face of all the earth. For after seven more days, I will send rain on the earth forty days and forty nights; and I will blot out from the face of the land every living thing that I have made." Noah did according to all that the Lord had commanded him."

Noah being seen as righteous was the only one that could bring redemption to all mankind. Jesus, likewise, was a righteous man that could bring redemption to all mankind. But not only was Noah a foreshadowing of Jesus, one could also argue that the ark was a foreshadowing of the cross.

Christopher Ness put it like this, "As Noah's self was a type of Christ, so was his ark, wherein alone salvation was found from that deluge of waters, accordingly in Christ alone can be found salvation (of all sorts, temporal, spiritual, and eternal) from the deluge of Divine wrath. and justice of God for the sin of man. Beside Him, there is no Saviour (Isaiah 43:11). As there was but one ark, so there must be but one mediator; no cock boats were to attend this ark (Acts 27:30)."

Jesus references the parallel between Himself and Noah in Matthew 24:35-39 when He says, ""But of that day and hour no one knows, not even the angels of heaven, nor the Son, but the Father alone. For the coming of the Son of Man will be just like the days of Noah. For as in those days before the flood they were eating and drinking, marrying and giving in marriage, until the day that Noah entered the ark, and they did not understand until the flood came and took them all away; so will the coming of the Son of Man be."

After the garden and the ark, the next place we see the redemptive work of Jesus foreshadowed in the Old Testament is in the story of Abraham and Isaac. Isaac was referenced as Abraham's only son in this story, even though he was the father of Ishmael as well, because Isaac was the son of the covenant. Abraham was thus asked to sacrifice his only son.

Genesis 22:9-14 describes the carrying out of this command when it says, "Then they came to the place of which God had told him; and Abraham built the altar there and arranged the wood, and bound his son Isaac and laid him on the altar, on top of the wood. Abraham stretched out his hand and took the knife to slay his son. But the angel of the Lord called to him from heaven and said, "Abraham, Abraham!" And he said, "Here I am." He said, "Do not stretch out your hand against the lad, and do nothing to him; for now I know that you fear God, since you have not withheld your son, your only son, from Me." Then Abraham raised his eyes and looked, and behold, behind him a ram caught in the thicket by his horns; and Abraham went and took the ram and offered him up for a burnt offering in the place of his son. Abraham called the name of that place The Lord Will Provide, as it is said to this day, "In the mount of the Lord it will be provided."

John Gill was referring to the ram found in the thicket when he said, "The Jewish writers say, it was from the creation of the world; and there is no absurdity or improbability to suppose it was immediately created by the power of God, and in an extraordinary manner provided; and was a type of our Lord Jesus, who was foreordained of God before the foundation of the world, and came into the world in an uncommon way, being born of a virgin, and that in the fulness of time, and seasonably, and in due time died for the sins of men."

Whether that ram was instantaneously created or whether it just wandered over from a neighboring area, the fact remains that God provided for Abraham and for Isaac. The parallels are many here, because Jesus became our sacrifice, when we should die for our sins Jesus takes the place instead. The faith of Abraham is only overshadowed here by the sovereignty of God.

Skipping ahead to the book of Exodus, Moses is also a foreshadowing of Jesus leading us to the Promised Land of Heaven. Moses delivered his people from slavery just as Jesus delivers us from the slavery of our sin. Moses held up the serpent to save his people, just as Jesus was raised up on the cross to save all people. God provided for the people bread from Heaven, Jesus is the bread of life.

Jesus mentioned the parallel between Himself and the manna from Heaven in John 6, "Our fathers ate the manna in the wilderness; as it is written, 'He gave them bread out of heaven to eat.'" Jesus then said to them, "Truly, truly, I say to you, it is not Moses who has given you the bread out of heaven, but it is My Father who gives you the true bread out of heaven. For the bread of God is that which comes down out of heaven, and gives life to the world." Then they said to Him, "Lord, always give us this bread." Jesus said to them, "I am the bread of life; he who comes to Me will not hunger, and he who believes in Me will never thirst."

Matthew Poole refers to the bread of life when he says, "the bread that giveth spiritual and eternal life, and the bread that upholdeth and maintains spiritual life; the Messiah, whom God hath sent into the world, to quicken those that are dead in trespasses and sins, Ephesians 2:1; and to give eternal life to as many as the Father hath given me."

The story of Moses and the Promised Land did not have a happy ending for Moses. God told Moses to speak to a rock and instead he struck it two times. God was not pleased. "Then Moses raised his arm and struck the rock twice with his staff. Water gushed out, and the community and their livestock drank. But the LORD said to Moses and Aaron, "Because you did not trust in me enough to honor me as holy in the sight of the Israelites, you will not bring this community into the land I give them."

Some point out that the rock might represent Christ who is often referred to as the rock. Some point to Moses' unbelief as the main point of the story. However, it could also be argued that in all the ways that Moses was a type of Christ, this way points directly to him being an antitype. Jesus was blameless and perfect when He came to this world. It was because of His perfect life that He was able to be the propitiation for our sin, die on the cross, and lead us to the Promised Land of Eternity.

Joshua then had to take upon himself the mantle of leadership and lead the people into the Promised Land. William Nicholson points out, "Joshua and Jesus have the same comprehensive meaning. The former in the Hebrew, and the latter in Greek, signify Savior. Joshua was so called, because eminently destined, and raised up to deliver Israel, and to conquer their enemies."

Nicholson also points out that besides just the name, there are a lot of other things that Jesus and Joshua have in common, "Joshua is called the servant of Moses, Exodus 24:13. By being a servant, he was prepared to become his successor. He was a faithful servant, obedient and submissive to the will of God. Just so, Jesus was first the servant of the law, before he procured the salvation of men. He became the servant of the ceremonial law before he abolished it. As to the moral law — he obeyed its precepts, and he endured its penalty. He "fulfilled all righteousness." As Joshua succeeded Moses, so Christ and his Gospel succeeded the whole Mosaic ritual. How superior the Gospel — how simple — how easy! "For the law was given through Moses; grace and truth came through Jesus Christ!" John 1:17"

The last Old Testament figure to point out, in reference to Jesus' redemption for all mankind being foreshadowed long ago, was actually spoken of by Jesus Himself. "Then some of the scribes and Pharisees said to Him, "Teacher, we want to see a sign from You." But He answered and said to them, "An evil and adulterous generation craves for a sign; and yet no sign will be given to it but the sign of Jonah the prophet; for just as Jonah was three days and three nights in the belly of the sea monster, so will the Son of Man be three days and three nights in the heart of the earth. The men of Nineveh will stand up with this generation at the judgment, and will condemn it because they repented at the preaching of Jonah; and behold, something greater than Jonah is here."

Charles Spurgeon was commenting on these verses when he said, "The great sign of our Lord's mission is his resurrection, and his preparing a gospel of salvation for the heathen. His life-story is well symbolized by that of Jonah. They cast our Lord overboard, even as the sailors did the man of God. The sacrifice of Jonah calmed the sea for the mariners, our Lord's death made peace for us. Our Lord was a while in the heart of the earth as Jonah was in the depth of the sea, but, he rose again, and his ministry was full of the power of his resurrection. As Jonah's ministry was certified by his restoration from the sea, so is our Lord's ministry attested by his rising from the dead. The man who had come back from death and burial in the sea commanded the attention of all Nineveh, and so does the risen Saviour demand and deserve the obedient faith of all to whom his message comes."

So as an overarching theme of the Bible we see that we are a people in desperate need of redemption. From the first sin, to the ark, to the sacrifice, to the wilderness, to the belly of a whale we see a common thread and that is of redemption and the need for someone to come and offer this redemption to all people. Jesus was that person, and He taught about as much constantly.

We have all racked up a huge debt. It is called a debt of sin. R.C. Sproul said "Both the Old and New Testaments make it clear that all human beings are sinners. As our sins are against an infinite, holy God who cannot even look upon sin, atonement must be made in order for us to have fellowship with God. Because sin touches even our best acts, we are incapable of making a sufficient sacrifice." The Ten Commandments was given to Moses back in the Old Testament as a means to measure ourselves against. But even if we kept those commandments, Jesus picked it up a notch in the Sermon on the Mount mentioned in a previous chapter.

In other words, we have all racked up a pretty big bill of sin. And some of us are better than others, and maybe some of you would say, "I have only done one thing on that list" That's fine but just one sin keeps us out of Heaven.

And Romans 6:23 says "The wages of sin is death . . ." This bill is going have to get paid for somehow. If you owe a bill, you will have to pay it somehow. If you can't pay the actual money then you will eventually have to pay with first your credit score and in the end some even see jail time, but someone has to pay your bills.

So we have two options here with our sin bill. Just like any other bill, we can pay for it ourselves, Remember Romans 6:23 says, "The wages of sin is death . . ." Or, we can let someone else pay for us. That is where the word propitiation comes in. Again I John 4:10 reads: "In this is love, not that we loved God, but that He loved us and sent His Son to be the propitiation for our sins."

So propitiation means this: It means to cover, to cancel, to appease. Let's say you are going out to a restaurant and someone says, "No, I'll cover you." It's happened to me a few times in my life where I will be at a restaurant and I will order, and someone will be with me who will order and it comes times to pay the bill and the waiter say, "Don't worry about it, someone paid for you." A couple of times in my life this has happened and the waiter will not tell me who it was, but will just say that paid for the tab. It's always the best dining experience. And this is a simplified version of the word "propitiation."

So I John 4:10 says "In this is love, not that we loved God, but that He loved us and sent His Son to be the propitiation for our sins." John is trying to explain to us what love is. This is love, we didn't love Him first, but He loved us so He sent us a propitiation for our debt. The word means: complete satisfaction. And this is what we got with the sacrificial death of Christ on the cross.

How is this possible? It is possible because 2 Cor. 5:21 says "He made Him who knew no sin to be sin on our behalf, so that we might become the righteousness of God in Him." It has been of this verse that, "Reconciliation between God and man is made possible by Christ's remedy for sin. "Made him to be sin" means at least that God the Son bore the consequences of sin. But it is a daring phrase that may mean much more. In some mysterious sense, the sinless Christ became identified with our sin so we could become identified with His righteousness."

Because Jesus knew no sin, He could pay the sin for us. Now imagine we are back at the restaurant and you're eating with me and someone mysteriously picks up my tab again. You back and forth with the waiter and he doesn't budge and you say, "Fine, if you won't tell me who paid, at least let me put 20 or 30 bucks toward the price of the meal." That would be ridiculous and pointless right? Why? Because you can't pay for a bill that has already been paid.

But some people try to do exactly that. We put money in the offering plate, read our Bible, etc. in an effort to subconsciously earn our salvation. You are trying to pay your sin bill with your righteousness but Isaiah 64:6 says "For all of us have become like one who is unclean, And all our righteous deeds are like a filthy garment; And all of us wither like a leaf, And our iniquities, like the wind, take us away."

Gary V. Smith said of this verse, "Sin had so pervaded their lives that even the things that most people would usually regard as righteous deeds were in fact more like filthy menstruation rags. This is an honest appraisal of the filthiness of sin, which is relatively rare in the past or today."

So we can't pay a bill that has already been paid, and surely can't pay a bill that is this high with filthy rags, it's not going to happen. The interesting thing is that in the Greek the word for propitiation is the same Greek word that you would use to describe The Mercy Seat. Let me rewind a couple thousand years and explore this a little more.

The Israelites were wandering through the wilderness and they made this portable tabernacle that they carried around with them. It had two sections: One where the priest sacrificed and then the Holy of Holies. It was the place where the God of Israel revealed Himself to and dwelled among His people. The basic Hebrew term (mishkan) translated as "tabernacle" (Exod. 25:9) comes from a verb that means "to dwell." In this sense it is correctly translated in some instances as "dwelling" "dwelling place," "habitation," and "abode."

In it was the Ark of the Covenant which was Solid Gold and had two cherubim angels with wings around the mercy seat. Cherubim angels represent judgment in the Bible as in when Adam and Eve were kicked out the garden, they guarded it with flaming swords.

Wings meant that judgment had been diverted from someone else to this Mercy Seat because this is where the blood of a goat was spilled. This is where the judgment of God was completely satisfied.

And the same Greek word used to describe the Mercy Seat is the word we talk about that is translated "propitiation." Meaning just like the blood on the Mercy Seat of God completely satisfied the sins of the nation of Israel, the blood Jesus shed for us on the cross completely satisfied the sin debt that we racked up.

And so finally let's look at I John 2:1-2 "1 My little children, I am writing these things to you so that you may not sin. And if anyone sins, we have an Advocate with the Father, Jesus Christ the righteous; 2 and He Himself is the propitiation for our sins; and not for ours only, but also for those of the whole world." Daniel Akin said in The New American Commentary in reference to propitiation that "John affirms that Jesus is the propitiation for the sins of the whole world. Since universal salvation is not an option (as seen above), this propitiation does not itself guarantee the actual salvation for the whole world. The provision for all has been accomplished. The reception and application of that provision is appropriated by faith."

We don't have to live in fear, we don't have to live in worry, we don't have to live in regret because Jesus Christ is the propitiation for our sins, for the whole world's!

Jesus Christ is the propitiation for all of our sins. He paid the debt we could not pay and I feel compelled to give my life to Him, not to help pay the debt, because the debt has already been paid. I am giving my life to Him in gratitude to the person who paid the debt I could not pay.

This what Jesus was teaching all those years ago, that He was to be the redemption for all mankind. This is why we know that Jesus is the greatest savior of all time.

CONCLUSION

Now What?

Sometimes, we think the same way for so long that it is difficult to see things from a different perspective. That's also true of spiritual truths. Jesus was passionate about helping us understand that the Kingdom of God is different than we might expect. Jesus said that the Kingdom of God was near.

If Jesus is truly the G.O.A.T., if He truly is the greatest of all time, what should we do with that information? What do we do now?

We go on mission.

The mission for all people that believe that Jesus is the G.O.A.T. is found in Acts 1:8 and it answers so many questions.

"But you will receive power when the Holy Spirit has come upon you; and you shall be My witnesses both in Jerusalem, and in all Judea and Samaria, and even to the remotest part of the earth."

These are words spoken by Jesus Himself. They are written in the book of Acts which was written by Luke as a continuation of his book that talked all about the life and ministry of Jesus.

Jesus gets crucified BUT He is resurrected, in other words, He is not dead. But for 40 days after he hung on a cross He would just randomly show up places. He was doing this so that people would know He is not dead, and even so that 2,000 years later we would know that He is not dead.

Right before He leaves Earth for the last time He has a discussion with His disciples that is chronicled right here in Acts 1.

Now let's just set the stage for a moment. You are a disciple of Jesus. Maybe not even one of the 12 (11 at this time) but around 100-120 people that were at least on the outside looking in.

Jesus came, Jesus was awesome, these people loved Jesus. Some of these people thought Jesus would be a mighty king. Some thought He would fix all of the problems of the day. And then they have to witness Him hanging on a cross in front of everyone for all to see. A gruesome, horrific death that no one should have to go through and it was someone they loved dearly.

Sad is not even an adequate word to describe the emotions of the day. Devastated, wrecked, sickened . . . I don't think these are strong enough words, but it is what we have.

Now think about what it must have been like to see Him again. He is standing right in front of you while you are deep in the mourning process. At first, you rub your eyes, check yourself . . . do all of the normal things to make sure you aren't going crazy. Then when it hits you that He really is standing in front of you everything changes.

But the problem is that He pops in and out; you never know where, you never know when. What a trip. So many different emotions! You don't want to go out to dinner because you just don't know if Jesus is going to pop by.

So here on this one particular popping in sequence we have the disciples talking to Jesus and still they didn't get it. They still were asking about Him restoring an earthly kingdom. And in Jesus' last statement to the disciples he said Acts 1:8 which was our mission and then "poof" He was gone. And the disciples were standing there with their mouths wide open.

So as Jesus gives us our mission the first thing He does is gives us power. The word power in the Greek is the word "dynamos" and it is where we get the word dynamite. Dynamite comes in, packs a mighty punch and changes the landscape of everything around it. You have the ability to do the exact same thing, because you have received this power as a follower of Jesus.

But what do you need power for? Maybe you have someone at your work or at your school and you don't have the courage to begin a spiritual conversation with them. You shall receive "dynamos."

Maybe you have a neighbor that no one talks to and you need to break through their rough exterior and introduce them to Jesus. You shall receive "dynamos."

Maybe it is as simple as inviting someone to church, but you are scared. You shall receive "dynamos." Jesus is telling His disciples, and He is telling us, that He has given us everything that we need to start a movement. You shall receive "dynamos."

And then it says you shall be my witnesses. For many years I was Michael Jordan's witness. I would go to school and tell everybody what I saw the night before on TV, when MJ stole a pass and made a breakaway dunk, or when he hit a game winning shot with his fade away jumper. I would tell people what I saw. That's what it means to be a witness.

Maybe you can understand it better like this. You are driving down the main road by your house and see two cars run into each other. You do what any good citizen does, you pull over to make sure everyone is okay. Then when the cops show up they ask you to stay around because they need a "witness" to what happened.

Now you don't get to tell the cop that you didn't go to criminal justice school so you cannot be a witness. You don't get to say that you didn't memorize the owner's manual of the car so you can't be a witness. You just tell the officer what you experienced. "I saw that car run into that car, and that car will never be the same again."

As a witness for Jesus, you don't have to have a theology degree and you don't have to have the Bible memorized. You just tell people what you experienced. "I ran into Jesus, and I will never be the same again." You can be a witness.

We do this every day. Television shows, sports moments, funny stories, etc. We are always telling people about what we saw and what we experienced, it is time to tell people that you saw and experienced the new king, one that can change their lives forever.

So the last question to answer is why? You always want to know the answer to that question. If the plan has been given and the power has been handed out and the places have been explained, the only question left to answer is . . . why? Why bother? Why do anything at all?

The answer is simple and sad and a bit stressful, there's no plan B. We are it! The plan to spread the name of Jesus to the world is all up to us. It was successfully shared by the 100 or so people that was here at Acts 1, so much so that I am writing a book about the greatness of Jesus because of their witness.

But honestly, if you don't tell your friends about Jesus . . . who will?

It was written in the red letters in your Bible, it was the famous last words of Jesus Himself. I think it is time that we get desperate for the mission. It is time that we get serious about letting everyone know that Jesus is the greatest of all time.

Jesus is the G.O.A.T.

ENDNOTES

1   Spurgeon, <u>Around the Wicket Gate: Help for those who only know About Christ</u>

2   Ryrie, New American Standard Bible

3   Ryrie, New American Standard Bible

4   Ryrie, New American Standard Bible

5   Jay Dennis, The Jesus Habits, 2005 (Nashville: Broadman and Holman Publishers)

6   Ryrie, New American Standard Bible

7   Ryrie, New American Standard Bible

8   Ryrie, New American Standard Bible

9   Philip Yancey, Prayer, 2006 (Grand Rapids: Zondervan, 2006)

10 Sproul, <u>What is Reformed Theology</u>

11 Ryrie, New American Standard Bible

12 Ryrie, New American Standard Bible

13 Strong, The New Strong's Exhaustive Concordance of the Bible

14 Strong, The New Strong's Exhaustive Concordance of the Bible

15 Ryrie, New American Standard Bible

16 Ryrie, New American Standard Bible

17 Strong, The New Strong's Exhaustive Concordance of the Bible

18 Ryrie, New American Standard Bible

19 Ryrie, New American Standard Bible

20 Henry, <u>Matthew Henry's Concise Commentary on the Whole Bible</u>

21 Henry, <u>Matthew Henry's Concise Commentary on the Whole Bible</u>

22 Lewis, <u>Mere Christianity</u>

23 Augustine, <u>Commentary on the Lord's Sermon on the Mount</u>

24 Crowe, <u>Sermons from the Mount</u>

25 Ryrie, New American Standard Bible

26 Calvin, <u>Calvin's Commentaries</u>

27 Ryrie, New American Standard Bible

28 Forest, <u>The Ladder of the Beatitudes</u>

29 Ryrie, New American Standard Bible

30 Webster's New World College Dictionary

31 Strong, The New Strong's Exhaustive Concordance of the Bible

32 Ryrie, New American Standard Bible

33 Edwards, <u>The Works of Jonathan Edwards</u>

34 Briscoe, <u>The Preacher's Commentary Series</u>

35 Thomas, <u>St. Thomas Aquinas Philosophical Texts</u>

36 Hunsinger, <u>Thy Word is Truth: Barth on Scripture</u>

37 Ryrie, New American Standard Bible

38 MacArthur, <u>The MacArthur Bible Commentary</u>

39 Barnes, <u>Barnes Notes on the Old and New Testaments</u>

40 Barnes, <u>Barnes Notes on the Old and New Testaments</u>

41 Ryrie, New American Standard Bible

42 Ryrie, New American Standard Bible

43 Ellicott, <u>Eliccott's Bible Commentary</u>

44 Ryrie, New American Standard Bible

45 Prioreschi, <u>A History of Medicine: Roman Medicine.</u>

46 Augustine, <u>Commentary on the Lord's Sermon on the Mount</u>

47   Ryrie, New American Standard Bible

48   Kruidenier, Holman new testament commentary

49   Ryrie, New American Standard Bible

50   Spurgeon, "The Shortest of the Seven Cries."

51   Ryrie, New American Standard Bible

52   Kruidenier, Holman new testament commentary

53   Ryrie, New American Standard Bible

54   Schreiner, New American commentary

55   Strong, The New Strong's Exhaustive Concordance of the Bible

56   Ryrie, New American Standard Bible

57   Ryrie, New American Standard Bible

58   Spurgeon, "The Shortest of the Seven Cries."

59   Ryrie, New American Standard Bible

60   Schreiner, New American commentary

61   Ryrie, New American Standard Bible

62   Schreiner, New American commentary

63   New King James Version. Copyright 1982 by Thomas Nelson, Inc.

64   Strong, The New Strong's Exhaustive Concordance of the Bible

65   Lewis, <u>Mere Christianity</u>

66   Webster's New World College Dictionary

67   Strong, The New Strong's Exhaustive Concordance of the Bible

68   Sinclair, <u>Hesiod, Works and Days</u>

69   Ryrie, New American Standard Bible

70   Tozer, <u>And He Dwelt Among Us: Teachings from the Gospel of John</u>

71   Ryrie, New American Standard Bible

72   MacArthur, <u>The MacArthur New Testament Commentary</u>

73   Tenney, <u>The Zondervan Encyclopedia of the Bible</u>

74   Ryrie, New American Standard Bible

75   Ryrie, New American Standard Bible

76   Ryrie, New American Standard Bible

77   Ryrie, New American Standard Bible

78   Ryrie, New American Standard Bible

79   Ryrie, New American Standard Bible

80   Lewis, <u>Mere Christianity</u>

81   Ryrie, New American Standard Bible

82   Maclarren, <u>Maclarren's Commentary of the Holy Scriptures</u>.

83   Price, <u>Handbook to the Baptist Hymnal</u>

84   Cruise, <u>Eusebius' Ecclesiastical History</u>: Complete and Unabridged

85   Durant, <u>Ceasar and Christ</u>

86   Ryrie, New American Standard Bible

87   Ryrie, New American Standard Bible

88   Graves, <u>The Twelve Ceasers</u>